Book 3

40 DAYS

God's Health Principles *for* His Last-Day *People*

DENNIS SMITH

REVIEW AND HERALD® PUBLISHING ASSOCIATION

Since 1861 | www.reviewandherald.com

Also by Dennis Smith:
40 Days: Prayers and Devotions to Prepare for the Second Coming (KJV Edition)
40 Days: Prayers and Devotions to Prepare for the Second Coming (NKJV Edition)
40 Days: Prayers and Devotions to Revive Your Experience With God (Book 2)

To order, call **1-800-765-6955**.
Visit us at **www.reviewandherald.com**
for information on other Review and Herald® products.

Copyright © 2011 by Review and Herald® Publishing Association

Published by Review and Herald® Publishing Association, Hagerstown, MD 21741-1119

Review and Herald® titles may be purchased in bulk for educational, business, fund-raising, or sales promotional use. For information, e-mail SpecialMarkets@reviewandherald.com.

The Review and Herald® Publishing Association publishes biblically based materials for spiritual, physical, and mental growth and Christian discipleship.

The author assumes full responsibility for the accuracy of all facts and quotations as cited in this book.

This book was
Edited by Gerald Wheeler
Copyedited by Jeremy J. Johnson
Designed by Ron J. Pride
Cover art by thinkstock.com
Typeset: Times New Roman 11.6/15.6

Texts credited to NIV are from the *Holy Bible, New International Version.* Copyright © 1973, 1978, 1984, International Bible Society. Used by permission of Zondervan Bible Publishers.

Verses marked TLB are taken from *The Living Bible,* copyright © 1971 by Tyndale House Publishers, Wheaton, Ill. Used by permission.

PRINTED IN U.S.A.

15 14 13 12   5 4 3 2

Library of Congress Cataloging-in-Publication Data
Smith, Dennis Edwin, 1944-   .
    40 days : prayers and devotions / Dennis Smith.
        p. cm.
    "Book 3"—Introd.
    1. Spiritual life—Seventh-Day Adventists. 2. Christian life—Adventist authors. 3. Second Advent—Prayers and devotions. 4. Seventh-Day Adventists—Prayers and devotions. I. Title. II. Title: Forty days.
    BV4501.3.S6462 2011
    248.4'86732—dc23
                        2011019711

ISBN 978-0-8280-2575-1

Contents

Introduction

This 40-days-of-study-and-prayer devotional, Book 3, is the third one in the series of 40-day devotionals. As with the first two 40-day devotionals, the present one seeks to get God's church ready for Christ's second coming as well as reach out to others in preparation for that glorious event. Such preparation begins with church members willing to commit to 40 days of prayer and devotional study to develop a closer personal relationship with Jesus Christ while reaching out to five individuals whom the Lord has put on their hearts to pray for every day.

Why Focus on Health?

The devotional studies in this book focus on the principles of health (physical, emotional, and spiritual) essential for God's people to understand and integrate into their lifestyle before the Second Coming. Ellen White wrote much on the subject of health and linked it with readying ourselves and others for Christ's return.

"In preparing a people for the Lord's second coming a great work is to be done through the promulgation of health principles. We are to relieve suffering by the use of the natural agencies that God has provided. We should teach the people how to prevent sickness by obedience to the laws of life, and while we work for the healing of the body we should seize every opportunity to work for the healing of the soul.

"This was Christ's method. He worked to restore both the physical and moral image of God in man. Both physical and moral health is to be communicated from the mighty Healer" (*Australasian Union Conference Record*, June 1, 1900).

The apostle Paul wrote: "I beseech you therefore, brethren, by the mercies of God, that ye present your bodies a living sacrifice, holy, acceptable unto God, which is your reasonable service. And be not conformed to this world: but be ye transformed by the renewing of your mind, that ye may prove what is that good, and acceptable, and perfect, will of God" (Rom. 12:1, 2).

Both the Old and New Testaments counsel us concerning our health. Satan knows that whatever affects our physical, emotional, and spiritual states of being will shape our relationship with God. Poor health habits will hinder us from being "transformed by the renewing of our mind" that the Lord desires to perform within us.

God communicates with us through our mind. Hence, anything that affects it will alter God's communication and influence in our life. Poor health habits will disturb the mental process and ultimately will limit God's ability to transform our lives. This devotional seeks to help readers better understand the laws of health in order to apply them in their life consistently and intelligently.

In the sections that present specific benefits of various lifestyle factors I have used several sources available through our denomination. The church has many good health and fitness programs available for use in a congregational and community setting. I would suggest you contact your conference health ministries director for more information on a health and fitness program that would be best fitted for your specific church.

Health ministry is to play a vital role in advanc-

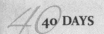

ing the gospel in preparation for Christ's second coming. Ellen White called it the right arm of the message.

"Again and again I have been instructed that the medical missionary work is to bear the same relation to the work of the third angel's message that the arm and hand bear to the body. Under the direction of the divine Head they are to work unitedly in preparing the way for the coming of Christ. The right arm of the body of truth is to be constantly active, constantly at work, and God will strengthen it. But it is not to be made the body. At the same time the body is not to say to the arm: 'I have no need of thee.' The body has need of the arm in order to do active, aggressive work. Both have their appointed work, and each will suffer great loss if worked independently of the other" (*Testimonies for the Church*, vol. 6, p. 288).

A Double Blessing

If you want to develop a closer relationship with Jesus in preparation for His soon return and reach out to those who have either once known the truth of God's Word and have slipped away, or have never known the warning message that He is giving to ready the world for Christ's soon return, then this 40 days of devotional studies and prayer is for you. Those on your prayer list may be family members, friends, coworkers, etc. They should be individuals living in your area in order to invite them to church sometime during the next 40 days. Write their names below,

1. _____

2. _____

3. _____

4. _____

5. _____

Pray for these individuals every day, claiming the scriptures below on their behalf (taken from *The Praying Church Sourcebook,* pp. 128, 129):
- that God will draw them to Himself (John 6:44).
- that they will seek to know God (Acts 17:27).
- that they believe the Word of God (1 Thess. 2:13).
- that Satan will be prevented from blinding them to the truth and that his influences in their life will be "cast down" (see 2 Cor. 4:4; 10:4, 5).
- that the Holy Spirit will work in them (John 16:8-13).
- that they turn from sin (Acts 3:19).
- that they believe in Christ as Savior (John 1:12).
- that they obey Christ as Lord (Matt. 7:21).
- that they take root and grow in Christ (Col. 2:6, 7).

Prayerfully consider the following suggestions to determine what the Lord wants you to do to reach out to those on your prayer list during the next 40 days. Add to this list as the Lord leads.

1. Call to express what you appreciate about them.
2. Mail a card sharing what God puts in your heart to tell them.
3. Send a piece of encouraging literature.
4. Call and pray with them.
5. Invite them to visit you in your home for a meal.
6. Invite them to go out to lunch with you.
7. Send a birthday card.
8. Send a card expressing encouragement.
9. Take them something that you have cooked or baked.
10. Invite them to accompany you shopping, on a trip to a museum, etc.
11. Send a get-well or sympathy card when needed.
12. Give their child a birthday card and gift when appropriate.
13. Invite them to attend church with you.
14. At the appropriate time, ask if they would like to receive Bible studies.
15. _____
16. _____

17. _____

18. _____

19. _____

20. _____

If your church plans a visitors' Sabbath and/or evangelistic meetings at the completion of the 40 days, be sure to invite those on your prayer list to such events.

Below is a suggested greeting when you contact those on your prayer list to inform them that you will be praying for them during the next 40 days. Then ask them what they want you to pray for. The 40 days will become a double blessing—blessing both you and those you reach out to.

Suggested Greeting for Prayer Contact

Hello, _____(interest's name)_____.
This is _____(your name)_____
My church is having a special emphasis on prayer and is requesting that we choose five individuals to pray for during the next 40 days. I have chosen you as one of my five to pray for.

What would you like for me to pray for especially in your behalf (such as family, job, a health issue, etc.)?

(Write down what they want you to pray for.)

I appreciate the opportunity to pray for your request during the next 40 days.

Thanks, _____(interest's name)_____;
I'll keep in touch.

Prayer's Central Role

Prayer is the most powerful force on earth. It is essential for one's own personal spiritual growth, and is the most effective means of reaching others for Christ. Concerning prayer and the Christian's spiritual growth Ellen White wrote:

"Prayer is the breath of the soul. It is the secret of spiritual power. No other means of grace can be substituted, and the health of the soul be preserved. Prayer brings the heart into immediate contact with the Well-spring of life, and strengthens the sinew and muscle of the religious experience. Neglect the exercise of prayer, or engage in prayer spasmodically, now and then, as seems convenient, and you lose your hold on God. The spiritual faculties lose their vitality, the religious experience lacks health and vigor" (*Gospel Workers*, pp. 254, 255).

She also recognized the necessity of prayer in leading others to Christ.

"Through much prayer you must labor for souls, for this is the only method by which you can reach hearts. It is not your work, but the work of Christ who is by your side, that impresses hearts" (*Evangelism,* p. 342).

"The Lord will hear our prayers for the conversion of souls" (*Messages to Young People,* p. 315).

As you consider the suggested ways to reach out to those you are praying for, you will not only be praying for them but also be working to bring them closer to Christ and His church. God will bless your efforts when you pray for and reach out to those on your prayer list. He will not only use you to win others to Christ but also draw you closer to Himself. Ellen White understood this double blessing when she wrote:

"As you work to answer your own prayers, you will find that God will reveal Himself unto you. . . . Begin now to reach higher and still higher. Prize the things of heaven above earthly attractions and inducements. . . . Learn how to pray; learn how to bear a clear and intelligent testimony, and God will be glorified in you" (*The Upward Look*, p. 256).

"Their persevering prayers will bring souls to the cross. In cooperation with their self-sacrificing efforts, Jesus will move upon hearts, working miracles in the conversion of souls" (*Testimonies for the Church*, vol. 7, pp. 27, 28).

In order to facilitate the prayer emphasis, you will find a Prayer Activity section at the end of each day's devotional. It gives a suggested prayer focus for the day related to the devotional subject for the day as well as those on your prayer list.

Fellowship

Christian fellowship is designed by God to assist His children in their victory over temptation and personal spiritual growth. We weren't created to stand alone. Paul commands us to pray for one another (Eph. 6:18). John tells us we are called by God to fellowship (1 John 1:3), and Christ said He was especially present when two or three believers fellowship together (Matt. 18:20). Therefore, it is highly recommended that you choose a fellow Christian to daily discuss the devotional with for that day, and pray for one another and for those you are reaching out to for Christ. This can be done via a phone call or in person.

Focus on the Baptism of the Holy Spirit

After His resurrection Jesus told His disciples that they were to wait to receive the baptism of the Holy Spirit before they went forth to proclaim the gospel to the world.

"And, being assembled together with them, commanded them that they should not depart from Jerusalem, but wait for the promise of the Father, which, saith he, ye have heard of me. For John truly baptized with water; but ye shall be baptized with the Holy Ghost not many days hence. . . . But ye shall receive power, after that the Holy Ghost is come upon you: and ye shall be witnesses unto me both in Jerusalem, and in all Judaea, and in Samaria, and unto the uttermost part of the earth" (Acts 1:4-8).

Even though they had spent the past three and a half years daily with Christ and had seen and participated in a ministry of miracles, they were not yet ready to witness for Him. They were to wait to receive the "power." After they experienced the baptism of the Holy Spirit, which took place on the day of Pentecost, they would be empowered as never before to witness for Christ.

"And when the day of Pentecost was fully come, they were all with one accord in one place. And suddenly there came a sound from heaven as of a rushing mighty wind, and it filled all the house where they were sitting. And there appeared unto them cloven tongues like as of fire, and it sat upon each of them. And they were all filled with the Holy Ghost, and began to speak with other tongues, as the Spirit gave them utterance" (Acts 2:1-4).

Because the baptism of the Holy Spirit, also called the infilling of the Spirit, is so vital to our personal spiritual growth and our witness to others, you will find this important teaching interwoven throughout the devotional studies. You will have opportunity to understand and experience better the biblical teaching about the baptism of the Holy Spirit as well as see its relationship to other vital biblical teachings.

By choosing to participate in the 40 days of study and prayer, you are entering into an amazing and blessed adventure with the Lord. You will experience a deeper relationship with Christ, your physical health will improve as you apply the health principles presented, and you will see the Lord use you to draw others closer to Himself in preparation for His soon return. As you fellowship with your prayer partner and the others participating in the 40 days of prayer and devotional study, you will gain a deeper Christian love and unity with your fellow believers, one that will also play an important role in your personal spiritual growth.

In order to get the most from the 40 days of study and prayer, we recommend that it be the first thing you do in the morning. It may require rising a little earlier, but the effort will be well rewarded. If you ask the Lord to wake you so you can have some quality time with Him, He will hear and answer your prayer. Concerning Christ's devotional life, Ellen White wrote:

"Daily He received a fresh baptism of the Holy Spirit. In the early hours of the new day the Lord awakened Him from His slumbers, and His soul and His lips were anointed with grace, that He might impart to others. His words were given Him fresh from the heavenly courts, words that He might speak in season to the weary and oppressed" (*Christ's Object Lessons,* p. 139).

Christ will do the same for you if you ask Him. He longs to anoint you with His Spirit in preparation for each new day. This 40-day devotional study is designed to facilitate just that—a daily anointing of God's Spirit for personal spiritual growth and witnessing for Christ.

Other Resources

If you are using this devotional study in preparation for a visitors' Sabbath and/or evangelistic meetings or health classes at the end of the 40 days, you should include those programs in the prayer focus each day. An instruction manual is available on the Web site www.40daysdevotional.com to help facilitate such a program in a church setting. Many congregations are employing this devotional book in this manner, and it is proving to be an effective spiritual preparation for evangelistic meetings, as well as a way to increase visitor attendance on those visitors' Sabbaths and evangelistic meetings held at the conclusion of the 40 days.

Note: Information on how to conduct a 40 Days program of devotional study and prayer in your church is available at www.40daysdevotional.com. It contains a free downloadable instruction manual.

The 40 Days devotionals are also prepared to work along with Light America Mission, a program of personal spiritual growth through study of God's Word and prayer, training, and community outreach to share the three angels' messages.

"*In* preparing a people for the Lord's second coming a great work is to be done through the pro-mulgation of health principles. We are to relieve suffering by the use of the natural agencies that God has provided. We should teach the people how to prevent sickness by obedience to the laws of life, and while we work for the healing of the body we should seize every opportunity to work for the healing of the soul."

(Australasian Union Conference Record, June 1, 1900).

Day 1

God's Plan for His Children

When God created human beings, He made them perfect in every way. The Lord had made a world that He declared was "very good" (Gen. 1:31), and then He placed the flawless couple in it. The world before sin knew no physical sickness, emotional problems, or spiritual weakness. All of these things came as the result of sin.

After sin entered our world through Adam and Eve's disobedience of God's revealed will, humanity developed physical diseases and damaged emotions, and became spiritually fallen, losing fellowship and enjoyment with God.

But the Lord had foreseen humanity's fall into sin and made provision for its total restoration physically, emotionally, and spiritually. God entered into the everlasting covenant whereby He laid out a plan of salvation that the Father, Son, and Holy Spirit would carry out in behalf of the human race. Christ would give Himself for humanity, enabling the human race to be redeemed. The Bible describes Christ's role in the plan of salvation devised before earth's creation as "the Lamb slain from the foundation of the world" (Rev. 13:8).

God has always desired only the best for His children. He wants us to be physically healthy, emotionally sound, and spiritually strong. And He has made it possible for those who believe in Christ to experience total restoration through Christ. Jesus said:

"The thief cometh not, but for to steal, and to kill, and to destroy: I am come that they might have life, and that they might have it more abundantly" (John 10:10).

Satan is the thief who stole humanity's physical, emotional, and spiritual health by leading it into sin. Jesus came to reverse what Satan had done by offering to the human race an abundant life. The apostle Paul supported what Jesus said when he wrote:

"And the very God of peace sanctify you wholly; and I pray God your whole spirit and soul and body be preserved blameless unto the coming of our Lord Jesus Christ. Faithful is he that calleth you, who also will do it" (1 Thess. 5:23, 24).

The apostle John said it this way:

"Beloved, I wish above all things that thou mayest prosper and be in health, even as thy soul prospereth" (3 John 2).

God has provided everything that His children need to experience the restoration that He desires to give them. However, many times the restitution is a cooperative one between Deity and humanity. For example, in the Old Testament God gave His people numerous health laws. Why did He do this? So that they would be healthy. He said:

"Wherefore it shall come to pass, if ye harken to these judgments, and keep, and do them. . . . Thou shalt be blessed above all people: there shall not be male or female barren among you, or among your cattle. And the Lord will take away from thee all sickness, and will put none of the evil diseases of Egypt, which thou knowest, upon thee" (Deut. 7:12-15).

The purpose of this 40-day devotional is to present how we are to cooperate with God in order to achieve the total physical, emotional, and spiritual renewal that He wants us to experience. In fact, those ready to meet Jesus when He returns will have undergone a total transformation, because Scripture tells us that they will be just like Jesus.

"Beloved, now are we the sons of God, and it doth not yet appear what we shall be: but we know that, when he shall appear, we shall be like him; for we shall see him as he is" (1 John 3:2).

Personal Reflection and Discussion

1. **What was humanity's condition physically, emotionally, and spiritually before sin entered our world?**

_____

_____

2. **What provision had God made to restore the human race after its fall into sin?**

_____

_____

3. **What kind of life did Jesus come to make available to His children?**

_____

_____

4. **What kind of restoration has God made possible for His children to experience?**

_____

_____

5. **What must we do to achieve the total renewal that God desires for us?**

_____

_____

Prayer Activity

Prayerfully consider what you can do to show you care for those on your prayer list.

Call each of them, telling them that you are praying for them, and ask them what they want you to pray for on their behalf.

Decide whom you want to be in fellowship with as you pray during the 40 days of prayer.

● **Call your prayer partner and discuss this devotional with him/her.**

● **Pray with your prayer partner:**

   (1) for God to bless you and your prayer partner as you study this devotional.

   (2) for God to enlighten you concerning how you are to cooperate with Him to achieve physically, emotionally, and spiritually the abundant life that He desires you to have.

   (3) for the individuals on your prayer list.

The Foundation of All Christian Growth and Health

Jesus was born of the Spirit, and "increased in wisdom and stature, and in favour with God and man" (Luke 2:52). When He reached the point in His life that He would face Satan's greatest temptations and begin His ministry, He sought another important experience with His Father. He prayed for and received the baptism of the Holy Spirit at His water baptism.

"Now when all the people were baptized, it came to pass, that Jesus also being baptized, and praying, the heaven was opened, and the Holy Ghost descended in a bodily shape like a dove upon him, and a voice came from heaven, which said, Thou art my beloved Son; in thee I am well pleased" (Luke 3:21, 22).

Jesus knew that the baptism of the Holy Spirit was essential in order to be victorious over every temptation that Satan attacked Him with, as well as to perform the ministry He came to carry out. The Spirit's infilling was so important to Jesus that Ellen White wrote:

"Daily He received a fresh baptism of the Holy Spirit. In the early hours of the new day the Lord awakened Him from His slumbers, and His soul and His lips were anointed with grace, that He might impart to others" (*Christ's Object Lessons,* p. 139).

The same experience is necessary for every Christian who wants to grow in God's grace and serve Him with an anointed ministry. Once Christ was filled with the Spirit, He was "led up of the Spirit into the wilderness to be tempted of the devil" (Matt. 4:1). Now He was ready for such temptations, and His first temptation involved appetite. It was the issue that had brought sin into the world: "And when the woman saw that the tree was good for food, and that it was pleasant to the eyes, and a tree to be desired to make one wise, she took of the fruit

thereof, and did eat, and gave also unto her husband with her; and he did eat" (Gen. 3:6). Christ began to gain the victory over sin for us by overcoming appetite.

"And when he had fasted forty days and forty nights, he was afterward an hungered. And when the tempter came to him, he said, If thou be the Son of God, command that these stones be made bread. But he answered and said, It is written, Man shall not live by bread alone, but by every word that proceedeth out of the mouth of God" (Matt. 4:2-4).

Christ is our example in all things. "For even hereunto were ye called: because Christ also suffered for us, leaving us an example, that ye should follow his steps" (1 Peter 2:21). We also must be filled with the Holy Spirit as Christ was if we are to triumph over appetite or any other temptation that Satan employs to weaken our physical, emotional, or spiritual condition. It is only through undergoing the baptism of the Holy Spirit daily that we receive the "fruit of the Spirit," which includes the fruit of "temperance" or self-control.

"But the fruit of the Spirit is love, joy, peace, longsuffering, gentleness, goodness, faith, meekness, temperance: against such there is no law" (Gal. 5:22, 23).

Hence, if we want to achieve the physical, emotional, and spiritual health that God desires us to have, we must constantly be filled with the Spirit. "And be not drunk with wine, wherein is excess; but be filled with the Spirit" (Eph. 5:18). The Greek verb form here for "be filled" is a continuous action verb meaning "keep on being filled." We must "keep on being filled" with God's Spirit so that we can "keep on receiving" His victory over Satan's temptations, and thus fulfill God's plan for all aspects of our health.

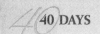

Personal Reflection and Discussion

1. How did Satan tempt Eve in order to bring sin into our world?

_____

_____

2. What experience did Jesus enter into in order to be prepared for His greatest temptations?

_____

_____

3. What was the first temptation that Satan used to try to get Jesus to sin?

_____

_____

4. Why do you think Satan employed that particular approach?

_____

_____

5. What experience in the Spirit must we have in order to be victorious over Satan's temptations, including appetite?

_____

_____

6. Why is the baptism of the Holy Spirit important for us to have victory over appetite?

_____

_____

Prayer Activity

- Call your prayer partner and discuss this devotional with him/her.
- Pray with your prayer partner:
    (1) for God to baptize you with His Holy Spirit.
    (2) for God to manifest all the fruit of the Spirit in your life.
    (3) for the individuals on your prayer list.

Receiving the Baptism of the Holy Spirit

Yesterday we saw the importance and even necessity of experiencing the baptism of the Holy Spirit in our lives in order to experience total health. God created human beings as multidimensional beings—physical, emotional, and spiritual. What affects one aspect will have an impact on all the others. Yielding to temptation will not only weaken us spiritually—it will negatively affect us physically and emotionally. We must receive the Spirit's infilling daily in order to experience the total restoration that He desires to give us. Also, the Spirit's infilling will enable us to develop Christ's character and have an anointed ministry for Jesus. That is why Jesus told His disciples to wait to be baptized in the Spirit.

"And, being assembled together with them, commanded them that they should not depart from Jerusalem, but wait for the promise of the Father, which, saith he, ye have heard of me. For John truly baptized with water; but ye shall be baptized with the Holy Ghost not many days hence. . . . But ye shall receive power, after that the Holy Ghost is come upon you: and ye shall be witnesses unto me both in Jerusalem, and in all Judaea, and in Samaria, and unto the uttermost part of the earth" (Acts 1:4-8).

The disciples did as Jesus said—they waited and prayed. Then on the tenth day, the Day of Pentecost, the Holy Spirit came and filled each of them.

"And when the day of Pentecost was fully come, they were all with one accord in one place. . . . And they were all filled with the Holy Ghost" (Acts 2:1-4).

Here we find the disciples receiving the baptism of the Holy Spirit in answer to prayer. The same was true of Jesus. Luke recorded that when Jesus was baptized in water, He prayed, and then the Holy Spirit came down and filled Him (Luke 3:21, 22).

After the day of Pentecost the baptism of the Holy Spirit was still essential for the believers. When Samaritans accepted Christ under Philip's preaching, Peter and John came to pray for them to receive the baptism of the Holy Spirit.

"But when they believed Philip preaching the things concerning the kingdom of God, and the name of Jesus Christ, they were baptized, both men and women. . . . Now when the apostles which were at Jerusalem heard that Samaria had received the word of God, they sent unto them Peter and John: Who, when they were come down, prayed for them, that they might receive the Holy Ghost: (For as yet he was fallen upon none of them: only they were baptized in the name of the Lord Jesus.) Then laid they their hands on them, and they received the Holy Ghost" (Acts 8:12-17).

We find a similar event in Saul's experience with Christ. Saul, who became the great apostle Paul, encountered the risen Christ on the road to Damascus. Then God sent him to a place to pray and wait. Next we read that God dispatched Ananias to go to Saul and pray for him.

"And Ananias went his way, and entered into the house; and putting his hands on him said, Brother Saul, the Lord, even Jesus, that appeared unto thee in the way as thou camest, hath sent me, that thou mightest receive thy sight, and be filled with the Holy Ghost. And immediately there fell from his eyes as it had been scales: and he received sight forthwith, and arose, and was baptized" (Acts 9:17, 18).

What was the result of Saul's Spirit-filled experience? He "increased the more in strength, and confounded the Jews which dwelt at Damascus, proving that this is very Christ" (verse 22). The future apostle to the Gentiles became stronger and stronger in the Lord.

This must be the experience of all who desire to be victorious through earth's final crisis and be ready for Christ's second coming. Spirit baptism is necessary for them to experience the physical, emotional, and spiritual health required to endure to the end.

Personal Reflection and Discussion

1. What did Jesus tell the disciples to wait for before they went forth to proclaim the gospel in power?

_____
_____

2. What did the disciples do in order to receive the baptism of the Holy Spirit on the day of Pentecost?

_____
_____

3. Why did Peter and John go to the newly baptized Samaritans?

_____
_____

4. Why did Ananias visit Saul?

_____
_____

5. Why was it important for the disciples, the Samaritans, and Saul to receive the baptism of the Holy Spirit?

_____
_____

6. Why is the baptism of the Holy Spirit necessary for God's last-day people?

_____
_____

Prayer Activity

● Call your prayer partner and discuss this devotional with him/her.
● Pray with your prayer partner:
    (1) for God to baptize you with His Holy Spirit.
    (2) for God to enable you to "increase the more in strength" in your life as Paul did.
    (3) for the individuals on your prayer list.

The Fruit of the Spirit

The focus of this 40-day devotional is health—physical, emotional, and spiritual. God created us multidimensional beings. We are physical, emotional, and spiritual creatures. In order to serve God effectively and be ready for Christ's return, we must be healthy in every area of life. The fruit of the Spirit covers all three dimensions.

"But the fruit of the Spirit is love, joy, peace, longsuffering, gentleness, goodness, faith, meekness, temperance: against such there is no law" (Gal. 5:22, 23).

The more of these fruits of the Spirit that we have in our life, the more we will reflect Christ's character. That is important because only those who mirror Jesus' character will be ready to meet Him. They have the Father's "name" in their foreheads, which is the character of Christ. "And I looked, and, lo, a Lamb stood on the mount Sion, and with him an hundred forty and four thousand, having his Father's name written in their foreheads" (Rev. 14:1).

Ellen White confirmed this when she wrote:

"Christ is waiting with longing desire for the manifestation of Himself in His church. When the character of Christ shall be perfectly reproduced in His people, then He will come to claim them as His own" (*Christ's Object Lessons,* p. 69).

An important question then is How do Christians receive the fruit of the Spirit? Through the baptism of the Holy Spirit. That is why the Spirit's infilling is so essential for physical, emotional, and spiritual wellness. A direct link exists between every fruit of the Spirit and our well-being.

For example, if I have love, joy, and peace in my heart, I will not be bitter toward anyone who has hurt me. It is essential for my spiritual health because the Bible says:

"Follow peace with all men, and holiness, without which no man shall see the Lord: Looking diligently lest any man fail of the grace of God; lest any root of bitterness springing up trouble you, and thereby many be defiled" (Heb. 12:14, 15).

If I don't have peace in my heart toward others, God's grace will have little effect in my life. Also, holding on to anger will negatively affect my physical and emotional condition.

Peter gave us another example. Anger at my wife negatively affects my relationship with God.

"Likewise, ye husbands, dwell with them according to knowledge, giving honour unto the wife, as unto the weaker vessel, and as being heirs together of the grace of life; that your prayers be not hindered" (1 Peter 3:7).

You see, the fruit of love, joy, and peace are essential in order to grow in Christ, experience the fullness of health, and be ready for Christ's second coming. The same is true of each of the other fruit of the Spirit. Therefore, it is essential that I ask God daily to fill me with His Spirit so that I can receive the fruit of the Spirit each day.

Ellen White understood this.

"When the Spirit of God takes possession of the heart, it transforms the life. Sinful thoughts are put away, evil deeds are renounced; love, humility, and peace take the place of anger, envy, and strife. Joy takes the place of sadness, and the countenance reflects the light of heaven" (*The Desire of Ages,* p. 173).

As the countenance "reflects the light of heaven"

total health will then result. "The religion of the Bible is not detrimental to the health of either body or mind. The influence of the Spirit of God is the very best medicine for disease. Heaven is all health; and the more deeply heavenly influences are realized, the more sure will be the recovery of the believing invalid. The true principles of Christianity open before all a source of inestimable happiness" (*Counsels on Health,* p. 28).

Personal Reflection and Discussion

1. In what ways are humans multidimensional beings?

_____

_____

2. What must we have in our life for us to be healthy in each area of it?

_____

_____

3. Describe how the fruit of the Spirit affect our spiritual dimension?

_____

_____

4. What will the physical, emotional, and spiritual dimensions in one's life being healthy do for the believer?

_____

_____

5. What did Ellen White say the baptism of the Holy Spirit did for the believer?

_____

_____

Prayer Activity

- **Call your prayer partner and discuss this devotional with him/her.**
- **Pray with your prayer partner:**
    (1) for God to baptize you with His Holy Spirit.
    (2) for God to fill you with the fruit of the Spirit in your life that you may fully reflect Him and experience total health.
    (3) for the individuals on your prayer list.

Christ's Presence

God has not left it up to His children by themselves to achieve the full restoration He desires for them. Christ not only came to this earth to gain the victory over sin that we need, and die the death that we deserve, but also is available to live in us in order to carry out the physical, emotional, and spiritual renewal in our lives that God desires for us. When He was about to leave earth, He told His disciples:

"And I will pray the Father, and he shall give you another Comforter, that he may abide with you for ever; even the Spirit of truth; whom the world cannot receive, because it seeth him not, neither knoweth him: but ye know him; for he dwelleth with you, and shall be in you. I will not leave you comfortless: I will come to you" (John 14:16-18).

Here Jesus promised to dwell in the believer. The living presence of Christ in the Christian became available on the day of Pentecost through the baptism of the Holy Spirit. Of this experience Ellen White wrote:

"The work of the Holy Spirit is immeasurably great. It is from this source that power and efficiency come to the worker for God; and the Holy Spirit is the comforter, as the *personal presence of Christ* to the soul. He who looks to Christ in simple, childlike faith, is made a partaker of the divine nature through the agency of the Holy Spirit. When led by the Spirit of God, the Christian may know that he is made complete in him who is the head of all things" (*Review and Herald,* Nov. 29, 1892; italics supplied).

Thus when we receive the baptism of the Holy Spirit, we gain the presence of Christ in our lives. In yesterday's devotional study we saw that the fruit of the Spirit are necessary for us to achieve the physical, emotional, and spiritual health that God wants us to have. Here we discover that in reality the fruit of the Spirit are actually the presence of Christ. We have dwelling in us His love, joy, peace, longsuffering (patience), gentleness, goodness, faith, meekness, and temperance (self-control) (Gal. 5:22, 23).

Christ is present in the Spirit-baptized believer. What the believer needs to learn is how to let Him live out His victory in the daily life. For example, when we are tempted to become impatient, our part is to turn our mind away from what seeks to cause us to be impatient, ask Christ to manifest His patience in us, and then believe that He will do so. Or, if we find ourselves wanting to be unforgiving toward others, we must turn our thoughts away from what those individuals did to cause us to become angry toward them, request Christ to display His forgiveness and compassion toward them, and then believe that He will do just that.

Therefore, the presence of Christ through the daily baptism of the Holy Spirit is necessary for us to experience the fruit of the Spirit in our life. And the fruit of the Spirit are mandatory for us to have the full restoration physically, emotionally, and spiritually that the Lord intends for us to possess.

The challenge we face is that certain physical habits, emotional attitudes, and spiritual neglect can hinder such transformation. That is why understanding the laws of our physical, emotional, and spiritual health are so important. In the area of physical disease, that is the very reason God connected obedience to His commands with freedom from sickness when He brought Israel out of their Egyptian captivity.

"Thou shalt therefore keep the commandments,

and the statutes, and the judgments, which I command thee this day, to do them. . . . And the Lord will take away from thee all sickness, and will put none of the evil diseases of Egypt, which thou knowest, upon thee" (Deut. 7:11-15).

In this devotional we will study the physical, emotional, and spiritual principles that we must understand and follow in order to experience the full health the Lord wants us to have and which is necessary to be ready for Christ's second coming.

Personal Reflection and Discussion

1. What experience in Christ does the baptism of the Holy Spirit bring to the believer?

_____

_____

2. What does Christ's presence provide for the believer?

_____

_____

3. Describe how the indwelling of Christ can give the believer victory over impatience?

_____

_____

4. Why did God give Israel laws concerning health, and what did He promise if His people followed them?

_____

_____

5. Why is it important that the Christian understand and follow God's revealed principles of health?

_____

_____

Prayer Activity

- **Call your prayer partner and discuss this devotional with him/her.**
- **Pray with your prayer partner:**
    (1) for God to baptize you with His Holy Spirit.
    (2) for God to help you to learn how to let Christ give you His victory when you are tempted.
    (3) for God to help you understand the principles of health in order to cooperate with Him in achieving physical, emotional, and spiritual wellness.
    (4) for the individuals on your prayer list.

Day 6

Worship—Part 1

When Christians think of worship they usually regard it as the act of attending church. In most people's minds worship involves going to some place to venerate God.

In the Old Testament the Jews worshipped God at the Temple in Jerusalem and later in synagogues. When in a distant land away from Jerusalem they prayed facing toward the Temple in Jerusalem. Such was Daniel's practice.

"Now when Daniel knew that the writing was signed, he went into his house; and his windows being open in his chamber toward Jerusalem, he kneeled upon his knees three times a day, and prayed, and gave thanks before his God, as he did aforetime" (Dan. 6:10).

The prophet did it because that was what God had instructed His people to do: "If thy people go out to battle against their enemy, whithersoever thou shalt send them, and shall pray unto the Lord toward the city which thou hast chosen, and toward the house that I have built for thy name: Then hear thou in heaven their prayer and their supplication, and maintain their cause" (1 Kings 8:44, 45).

During King Jehoiakim's reign God told the prophet Jeremiah: "Thus saith the Lord; Stand in the court of the Lord's house, and speak unto all the cities of Judah, which come to worship in the Lord's house, all the words that I command thee to speak unto them; diminish not a word" (Jer. 26:2).

In the New Testament we find a different concept of worship. Instead of regarding it as going to some place to honor and praise God, worship is closely linked to obedience in the life. John recorded a conversation that Jesus had with the woman at the well. In it Christ and the woman discussed worship. The woman said to Jesus:

"Our fathers worshipped in this mountain; and ye say, that in Jerusalem is the place where men ought to worship. Jesus saith unto her, Woman, believe me, the hour cometh, when ye shall neither in this mountain, nor yet at Jerusalem, worship the Father. Ye worship ye know not what: we know what we worship: for salvation is of the Jews. But the hour cometh, and now is, when the true worshippers shall worship the Father in spirit and in truth: for the Father seeketh such to worship him. God is a Spirit: and they that worship him must worship him in spirit and in truth" (John 4:20-24).

Jesus indicated that worship involved obeying the truths of God in one's life: "True worshippers shall worship the Father in spirit and in truth" (verse 23). The apostle Paul taught the same concept of worship when he wrote:

"Whether therefore ye eat, or drink, or whatsoever ye do, do all to the glory of God" (1 Cor. 10:31).

Paul explained that everything we do is an act of worship, including what we eat and drink. Therefore, when we are following God's health principles by eating and drinking according to His revealed will we are actually worshipping Him.

Worship involves representing God correctly and acknowledging His proper position in our life and in the world. That is why He said not to worship Him using images and idols. Idols totally misrepresent God.

"Thou shalt not make unto thee any graven image, or any likeness of any thing that is in heaven above, or

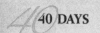

that is in the earth beneath, or that is in the water under the earth. Thou shalt not bow down thyself to them, nor serve them" (Ex. 20:4, 5).

Therefore, when Paul states that we are to eat and drink to God's glory, he is acknowledging that as we do so in harmony with God's will we are properly representing Him to the world. Thus to eat and drink according to divine instruction is an act of worship and glorifying God.

Personal Reflection and Discussion

1. How did the Jews worship God in the Old Testament?

_____

_____

2. Toward what location did Daniel pray?

_____

_____

3. How did Jesus define true worship?

_____

_____

4. What does it mean to worship God in spirit and truth?

_____

_____

5. What did Paul say about worship and glorifying God?

_____

_____

6. What does what we eat and drink have to do with worship?

_____

_____

Prayer Activity

● **Call your prayer partner and discuss this devotional with him/her.**
● **Pray with your prayer partner:**
    (1) for God to baptize you with His Holy Spirit.
    (2) for God to help you to understand and apply His health principles so that you can worship and glorify Him even more in your life.
    (3) for the individuals on your prayer list.

Worship—Part 2

In yesterday's devotional we saw that in the New Testament worship involves everything we do. We venerate God by obeying His revealed will. Thus when we follow God's health principles we are actually worshipping Him.

In the Old Testament worship involved offering sacrifices to God. The Lord had instructed Israel concerning several different sacrifices that He would accept for worship. From the very beginning the proper sacrifice was important, because it revealed one's attitude toward God. It indicated whether the worshipper respected and reverenced Him by obeying His instruction or not.

We see this issue in the worship of God by Cain and Abel. Abel paid homage to the Lord with a sacrifice according to His revealed will. Cain did not. Scripture tells how God viewed the two men's worship of Him.

"And in process of time it came to pass, that Cain brought of the fruit of the ground an offering unto the Lord. And Abel, he also brought of the firstlings of his flock and of the fat thereof. And the Lord had respect unto Abel and to his offering: But unto Cain and to his offering he had not respect" (Gen. 4:3-5).

Here we see that how we worship God is a serious matter in His sight. Cain disregarded the Lord's instruction to come before Him in worship with an animal sacrifice.

The Old Testament animal sacrificial system ended at the cross. Jesus is our sacrificial lamb today. However, the New Testament states that we are to still bring to God a sacrifice: not an animal but our own selves—our bodies.

"I beseech you therefore, brethren, by the mercies of God, that ye present your bodies a living sacrifice, holy, acceptable unto God, which is your reasonable service" (Rom. 12:1).

God has clearly explained the sacrifice we are to offer Him today. We are to present our bodies to Him as a living sacrifice.

What does this say about the condition our bodies are to be in when we offer them to God? In the Old Testament the animal sacrificed was to be without blemish (Ex. 12:5). God was to receive only the very best.

Thus we must present our bodies to God in the very best condition possible. To offer anything less is to show Him disrespect and actually worship Him in a manner similar to that of Cain. Therefore, we must take God's health counsels seriously. Our health habits will play a major role in the kind of body we bring to Him.

With this understanding of true worship and the sacrifice that we are to offer to God, we can better grasp why it is important we become informed on the laws of our being and apply them to our everyday living.

The last-day three angels of Revelation summon God's people to "worship him that made heaven, and earth, and the sea, and the fountains of waters" (Rev. 14:7). Those ready to meet Jesus will be worshipping God in spirit and truth as Jesus said (John 4:24) and will "present [their] bodies a living sacrifice to God" (Rom. 12:1). God will honor their worship of Him and bless them with good health. Their health will be an important factor in their victory and faithfulness to Jesus during the final crisis on earth.

Personal Reflection and Discussion

1. Why did God accept Abel's offering and not Cain's?

_____

_____

2. How important is it to God how we worship Him?

_____

_____

3. What is the sacrifice that the New Testament tells us that we should bring to God?

_____

_____

4. What does the teaching that we are to present our bodies as a living sacrifice to God indicate about the condition our bodies should be in?

_____

_____

5. What role do God's health laws play in our sacrificial offering to God today?

_____

_____

6. Do you think one's health will be important just before Jesus comes?

_____

_____

Prayer Activity

● Call your prayer partner and discuss this devotional with him/her.

● Pray with your prayer partner:

    (1) for God to baptize you with His Holy Spirit.

    (2) for God to help you to understand how you can present your body as a living sacrifice to Him.

    (3) for the individuals on your prayer list.

A Holy People

The Old Testament depicts holy places and holy objects. The wilderness tabernacle was so important to God that He gave very specific instructions about its construction and the manufacture of the articles in it. After all, the sanctuary or wilderness tabernacle was to be God's special place on earth.

"And let them make me a sanctuary; that I may dwell among them. According to all that I shew thee, after the pattern of the tabernacle, and the pattern of all the instruments thereof, even so shall ye make it" (Ex. 25:8, 9).

The ark, which contained the Ten Commandments that God had given to Moses, was so holy that only the Levites could touch it, as we see illustrated in an incident that took place when King David brought it to Jerusalem.

"And when they came to Nachon's threshingfloor, Uzzah put forth his hand to the ark of God, and took hold of it; for the oxen shook it. And the anger of the Lord was kindled against Uzzah; and God smote him there for his error; and there he died by the ark of God" (2 Sam. 6:6, 7).

Years later, when the Jews were captive in Babylon because of their sin, the Babylonian king Belshazzar used the holy articles taken from God's Temple in Jerusalem in a most unholy manner.

"Belshazzar the king made a great feast to a thousand of his lords, and drank wine before the thousand. Belshazzar, whiles he tasted the wine, commanded to bring the golden and silver vessels which his father Nebuchadnezzar had taken out of the temple which was in Jerusalem; that the king, and his princes, his wives, and his concubines, might drink therein. Then they brought the golden vessels that were taken out of the temple of the house of God which was at Jerusalem; and the king, and his princes, his wives, and his con-cubines, drank in them" (Dan. 5:1-3).

That very night God's wrath fell on the king. Cyrus, the Medo-Persian general, led his armies into Babylon, and Belshazzar perished.

The New Testament does not speak of holy places or vessels. God no longer resides in a building on earth. Rather, He dwells in His people. That is why Scripture calls His people the temple of God. "Know ye not that ye are the temple of God, and that the Spirit of God dwelleth in you?" (1 Cor. 3:16).

Because the Christian is God's holy temple, we are to do nothing that will desecrate our body temple. Anything we do that will harm us is a sin in His sight. God takes desecration of His temple today just as seriously as He did in the Old Testament.

"If any man defile the temple of God, him shall God destroy; for the temple of God is holy, which temple ye are" (1 Cor. 3:17).

Believers in Jesus Christ who have the Spirit of God dwelling in them are God's temple on earth. Today, instead of holy places or holy vessels on earth, there is only a "holy people." Peter describes God's people as "a chosen generation, a royal priesthood, an holy nation, a peculiar people; that ye should shew forth the praises of him who hath called you out of darkness into his marvellous light" (1 Peter 2:9). The apostle then goes on to counsel us: "Dearly beloved, I beseech you as strangers and pilgrims, abstain from fleshly lusts, which war against the soul" (verse 11).

We are God's holy dwelling place. Therefore, we need to take seriously His counsels concerning how to care for His temple. We should seek to be undefiled physically, emotionally, and spiritually by following the health laws established by God.

Personal Reflection and Discussion

1. List some of the holy places and vessels in the Old Testament.

_____

_____

2. How did God regard misuse of His holy vessels?

_____

_____

3. Do we find holy places and vessels on earth in the New Testament?

_____

_____

4. What is the holy place of God on earth in the New Testament?

_____

_____

5. What does knowing that we are the holy temple of God teach us about how we are to take care of our body temple?

_____

_____

6. Do you think how we take care of our body temple is important to God?

_____

_____

Prayer Activity

● **Call your prayer partner and discuss this devotional with him/her.**
● **Pray with your prayer partner:**
    (1) for God to baptize you with His Holy Spirit.
    (2) for God to help you to be an acceptable dwelling place for Him.
    (3) for the individuals on your prayer list.

Good Stewards

Two important concepts are ownership and stewardship. When we own something, we have the right to do with it as we please as long as we don't use it to commit a crime. When we are a steward or custodian of someone else's property, we must care for it according to the owner's directions.

Society today has the attitude that we can do whatever we want as long as no one gets hurt. The feeling is "I am free to eat what I want, drink what I want, and live any lifestyle I want." Unfortunately, such an attitude has led to much heartache and difficulty in the areas of moral behavior, health, family breakdown, etc. Everyone seems to want to be a law unto themselves. It reminds us of God's people in the book of Judges, which declared that "every man did that which was right in his own eyes" (Judges 17:6). Such a mind-set is that of ownership, not stewardship.

The Bible teaches a quite different principle of life. Scripture pictures humanity as belonging to God. The Lord created the human race and thus is its owner. As owner, God has the right to instruct human beings in their lifestyle and activities.

When I became a Christian, I found such an idea a totally new concept. I viewed religion as a once-a-week matter. Go to church once a week, and then spend your time as you choose the rest of the week. Then as I studied God's Word I discovered that God has instruction for His children in every area of their life: what they eat, how they dress, their entertainments, how they use their money—the list could go on and on.

The Bible not only teaches that God owns us by virtue of creating us but also because He redeemed us from sin.

"For ye are bought with a price: therefore glorify God in your body, and in your spirit, which are God's" (1 Cor. 6:20).

God paid the ultimate price for us—Christ's sacrifice. Because of this Paul wrote:

"For he that is called in the Lord, being a servant, is the Lord's freeman: likewise also he that is called, being free, is Christ's servant. Ye are bought with a price; be not ye the servants of men" (1 Cor. 7:22, 23).

We are to be servants of Christ, obeying Him in all our ways. Thus we must consider ourselves as stewards of God, not owners of ourselves to do whatever we please. Paul wrote:

"Moreover it is required in stewards, that a man be found faithful" (1 Cor. 4:2).

As a result, Christians must take seriously the instruction that God gives concerning how to take care of the body that God has given them. Whenever we follow God's health laws we are being good stewards. But whenever we disregard His health laws we are being unfaithful stewards.

Jesus told a parable about the talents that God has given us and the use we make of them. Everything we have is considered a talent—our money, voice, abilities, body, etc. To the ones who used their talents according to the master's instruction, "his lord said unto him, Well done, good and faithful servant; thou hast been faithful over a few things, I will make thee ruler over many things: enter thou into the joy of thy lord" (Matt. 25:23). But to the one who did not follow his master's instruction, "his lord answered and said unto him, Thou wicked and slothful servant. . . . Cast ye the unprofitable servant into outer darkness: there shall be weeping and gnashing of teeth" (verses 26-30).

The Bible is clear. As God's stewards and servants we are to take seriously what He has to say about the laws of our being. We are to do our best to attain physical, emotional, and spiritual health, which are an essential part of being a faithful steward and servant of God. This will also be the attitude those have who are ready for Christ's return.

Personal Reflection and Discussion

1. What is the difference between an owner and a steward?

_____

_____

2. What is the popular attitude today concerning stewardship?

_____

_____

3. Why does God have the right to ask us to care for our bodies?

_____

_____

4. If we disregard God's instruction about caring for our bodies physically, emotionally, and spiritually, what kind of steward or servant are we?

_____

_____

5. What did Jesus say would happen to unfaithful servants?

_____

_____

Prayer Activity

- **Call your prayer partner and discuss this devotional with him/her.**
- **Pray with your prayer partner:**
    (1) for God to baptize you with His Holy Spirit.
    (2) for God to help you to be a faithful steward and servant for Him.
    (3) for the individuals on your prayer list.

I am not much of a handyman when it comes to fixing things. I have known of some individuals who can repair almost anything. I wish I were more that way. However, whenever I pick up a tool to fix anything, I want that tool to be in good working condition. For example, if I need to use a crescent wrench and find that the mechanism is rusty so that I cannot adjust it, that tool will be of little use to me. I need tools that are in good working condition.

Should you require surgery for some health problem, you would expect the physicians to have good instruments to use in the procedure. You don't want surgeons to operate with dull scalpels. They may be the best in the world for a particular specialty, but not having good instruments will greatly limit their effectiveness.

The same is true of God. Perfect in all His ways, He is able to do marvelous things on earth. However, He has made Himself dependent on human beings to carry out His will through them. When Jesus saw how ready and needy the world was for salvation, He asked His disciples to "pray ye therefore the Lord of the harvest, that he will send forth labourers into his harvest" (Matt. 9:38). He has chosen to work through His human followers.

God has promised to fill us with His presence by the Holy Spirit. For Jesus said He would live in us through the baptism of the Holy Spirit.

"And I will pray the Father, and he shall give you another Comforter, that he may abide with you for ever; even the Spirit of truth; whom the world cannot receive, because it seeth him not, neither knoweth him: but ye know him; for he dwelleth with you, and shall be in you. I will not leave you comfortless: I will come to you" (John 14:16-18).

That is why Jesus said: "Verily, verily, I say unto you, He that believeth on me, the works that I do shall he do also; and greater works than these shall he do; because I go unto my Father" (verse 12). The works we do are to be Jesus doing them in and through us. We are to be "instruments of righteousness" (Rom. 6:13) in God's hands.

We can also use the analogy of musical instruments. If they are out of tune, the musicians will not be able to perform at their best no matter how well they have mastered the instruments.

The same is true of God using Christians. He wants to use us to bless others and advance His work. However, if we have weakened our bodies by poor health habits, dulled our minds by intemperance, and are spiritually weak because of poor spiritual practices, we will be of little use to Him. God will not be able to play the most beautiful music in and through our lives, because our lives will be out of tune with Him.

Therefore, we must take seriously God's counsels concerning our physical, emotional, and spiritual health. Only then will we be effective instruments in His hands. And only then will we glorify His name to the utmost. That is why Paul wrote:

"Whether therefore ye eat, or drink, or whatsoever ye do, do all to the glory of God" (1 Cor. 10:31).

Personal Reflection and Discussion

1. What kind of tool do you want to use when trying to repair something?

_____

_____

2. How dependent is God on human beings for carrying out His work on earth?

_____

_____

3. What are you to be in God's hands?

_____

_____

4. Why is it important that you be physically, emotionally, and spiritually healthy for God to be able to use you?

_____

_____

5. According to Paul, what principle should be at the center of our thinking in the area of what we eat, drink, etc.?

_____

_____

Prayer Activity

- **Call your prayer partner and discuss this devotional with him/her.**
- **Pray with your prayer partner:**
    - **(1) for God to baptize you with His Holy Spirit.**
    - **(2) for God to help you to be an effective instrument in His hands by following His instruction concerning your physical, emotional, and spiritual health.**
    - **(3) for the individuals on your prayer list.**

Day 11

Spiritual Diet—Bible Study

God's desire for His children is that they be spiritually healthy. Just as we must have the right kinds of food for physical health, so also we need proper spiritual food for spiritual health. The Bible is the best spiritual food there is.

If we neglect to study God's Word, we will be faithless, feel self-righteous, live a defeated Christian life, lack wisdom and discernment, have no real joy or peace, and will fail to receive eternal life. We find God's power in His Word.

"For the word of God is quick, and powerful, and sharper than any twoedged sword, piercing even to the dividing asunder of soul and spirit, and of the joints and marrow, and is a discerner of the thoughts and intents of the heart" (Heb. 4:12).

Ellen White wrote the following about God's Word, the Bible.

"The creative energy that called the worlds into existence is in the word of God. This Word imparts power; it begets life. Every command is a promise; accepted by the will, received into the soul, it brings with it the life of the Infinite One. It transforms the nature and re-creates the soul in the image of God" (*Education,* p. 126).

It is through God's Word that one is born again and experiences sanctification. "Being born again, not of corruptible seed, but of incorruptible, by the word of God, which liveth and abideth for ever" (1 Peter 1:23). "Sanctify them through thy truth: thy word is truth" (John 17:17).

Peter further describes God's sanctifying power in the life.

"Whereby are given unto us exceeding great and precious promises: that by these ye might be partakers of the divine nature, having escaped the corruption that is in the world through lust" (2 Peter 1:4).

If we neglect study of God's Word, we will not grow spiritually into Christlikeness. Also, our faith will be weak, because it can increase only as we expose ourselves to God's Word. "So then faith cometh by hearing, and hearing by the word of God" (Rom. 10:17).

Knowledge of God's Word will affect our prayer life. It increases our faith in prayer and brings to our understanding God's will so that we can have assurance that He will answer our prayers.

"And this is the confidence that we have in him, that, if we ask any thing according to his will, he heareth us: And if we know that he hear us, whatsoever we ask, we know that we have the petitions that we desired of him" (1 John 5:14, 15).

"In every command and in every promise of the Word of God is the power, the very life of God, by which the command may be fulfilled and the promise realized. He who by faith receives the Word is receiving the very life and character of God" (*Christ's Object Lessons,* p. 38).

To obtain good spiritual health, we must take time every day to feed on God's Word. Good spiritual health will have a positive effect on our physical and emotional health as well. "Beloved, I wish above all things that thou mayest prosper and be in health, even as thy soul prospereth" (3 John 2).

Note that John recognized a powerful connection between the condition of our soul and our health. God created us multidimensional beings. What affects one area has an impact on the rest, either for good or for bad.

A clear knowledge of God's Word will be an essential shield against Satan's last-day deceptions. "Only those who have been diligent students of the Scriptures, and who have received the love of the truth, will be shielded from the powerful delusion that takes the world captive" (*The Faith I Live By,* p. 346).

Personal Reflection and Discussion

1. What is the best spiritual food that one can feast on?

_____

_____

2. What will happen to our spiritual life if we neglect to study the Bible?

_____

_____

3. What benefits do we receive when we study the Bible?

_____

_____

4. How will Bible study affect our prayer life?

_____

_____

5. How did John connect our spiritual prosperity with our physical health?

_____

_____

6. What did Ellen White say about the necessity of being diligent students of God's Word?

_____

_____

Prayer Activity

● **Call your prayer partner and discuss this devotional with him/her.**
● **Pray with your prayer partner:**
    (1) for God to baptize you with His Holy Spirit.
    (2) for God to help you to take time every day in study of His Word so that you can grow in spiritual, physical, and emotional health.
    (3) for the individuals on your prayer list.

Day 12

Spiritual Fresh Air
—Prayer

Just as studying God's Word is our spiritual food, praying is the fresh spiritual air that we are to breathe. Should we neglect taking time to pray every day, we would not be spiritually healthy. If we do not pray, we will not advance in our Christian life, our service for the Lord will be fruitless, we will have little power in our life and service, and we will not be ready for earth's final crisis and Christ's second coming. Ellen White wrote of the necessity of prayer.

"Prayer is the breath of the soul. It is the secret of spiritual power. No other means of grace can be substituted, and the health of the soul be preserved. Prayer brings the heart into immediate contact with the Wellspring of life, and strengthens the sinew and muscle of the religious experience. Neglect the exercise of prayer, or engage in prayer spasmodically, now and then, as seems convenient, and you lose your hold on God. The spiritual faculties lose their vitality, the religious experience lacks health and vigor" (*Gospel Workers,* pp. 254, 255).

Praying Christians are men and women of power. The early church and disciples were men and women of prayer. Luke records: "And they continued steadfastly in the apostles' doctrine and fellowship, and in breaking of bread, and in prayers" (Acts 2:42).

God delights to answer the prayers of His children. "And call upon me in the day of trouble: I will deliver thee, and thou shalt glorify me" (Ps. 50:15).

Most Christians pray little because of being too busy or too tired. We need to realize the necessity and power of prayer. Prayer releases divine power. At Creation God established the principle that He carries out His will on earth through His human creation, not independent from them. When God seeks to accomplish something, He will convict His children to pray for the very thing He wants to do. That is why Jesus said that we should pray to the Father, "Thy kingdom come, Thy will be done in earth, as it is in heaven" (Matt. 6:10).

For example, when God told Elijah it was His will that Israel experience a drought because of their sin during the time of King Ahab, the prophet knew that he had to pray for God's will to be done. Then when God told him that He wanted rain to return, Elijah prayed that it would rain.

"Elias was a man subject to like passions as we are, and he prayed earnestly that it might not rain: and it rained not on the earth by the space of three years and six months. And he prayed again, and the heaven gave rain, and the earth brought forth her fruit" (James 5:17, 18).

The Bible records that Elijah had to pray seven times before the rain finally fell. Concerning the necessity of Elijah's persevering prayer for rain Ellen White wrote: "Had he given up in discouragement at the sixth time, his prayer would not have been answered, but he persevered till the answer came" (*The Seventh-day Adventist Bible Commentary,* Ellen G. White Comments, vol. 2, p. 1034).

History confirms the truth that men and women of prayer have been mighty in God's service. Satan does not fear our organization, planning, and methods. But he does tremble before our prayers.

The devil sought Peter's destruction. The Spirit made Christ aware of his plans, and Christ knew immediately what to do, as He explained to Peter:

"Simon, Simon, behold, Satan hath desired to have you, that he may sift you as wheat: but I have prayed for thee, that thy faith fail not: and when thou art converted, strengthen thy brethren" (Luke 22:31, 32).

If we want to be victorious Christians who are strong in faith and bring glory to God in our life, we must be men and women of prayer. That means we must maintain a moment-by-moment, prayerful connection with God. We must "pray without ceasing" (1 Thess. 5:17).

"Unless we become vitally connected with God, we can never resist the unhallowed effects of self-love, self-indulgence, and temptation to sin. We may leave off many bad habits, for the time we may part company with Satan; but without a vital connection with God, through the surrender of ourselves to Him moment by moment, we shall be overcome. Without a personal acquaintance with Christ, and a continual communion, we are at the mercy of the enemy, and shall do his bidding in the end" (*The Desire of Ages,* p. 324).

Personal Reflection and Discussion

1. What is prayer compared to in the physical world?

_____

_____

2. What will happen to our spiritual life if we neglect prayer?

_____

_____

3. What benefits do we receive when we pray?

_____

_____

4. What must we do for God's will to be done in our life and in the world?

_____

_____

5. Is prayer in the morning all the prayer that we need? Why or why not?

_____

_____

Prayer Activity

- **Call your prayer partner and discuss this devotional with him/her.**
- **Pray with your prayer partner:**
    - **(1) for God to baptize you with His Holy Spirit.**
    - **(2) for God to help you to pray every day and maintain a prayerful connection with Him in order to grow in spiritual, physical, and emotional health.**
    - **(3) for the individuals on your prayer list.**

Day 13
Spiritual Exercise —Witnessing

As personal Bible study is analogous to eating and prayer is similar to breathing in the physical realm, so sharing our faith benefits our spiritual well-being just as exercise strengthens the physical body. Just as one who does not exercise will become weak and sickly, so also one who does not extend his or her faith to others will become spiritually feeble.

Paul clearly understood the necessity of witnessing for Christ when he wrote: "That if thou shalt confess with thy mouth the Lord Jesus, and shalt believe in thine heart that God hath raised him from the dead, thou shalt be saved. For with the heart man believeth unto righteousness; and with the mouth confession is made unto salvation" (Rom. 10:9, 10).

It is vital that Christians share their faith. It can be done in numerous ways and places—in the family, with friends, even with strangers as the opportunity arises. We need to ask the Lord every day to lead us into situations in which we can witness to our faith in Him. Then we must be sensitive to His leading, and the Spirit's conviction to present Christ when He opens the way for us to speak in His behalf.

Jesus has given us His own example of the most effective way to witness for Him.

"Christ's method alone will give true success in reaching the people. The Savior mingled with men as one who desired their good. He showed His sympathy for them, ministered to their needs, and won their confidence. Then He bade them, 'Follow Me'" (*Gospel Workers,* p. 363).

We must show genuine interest in others. The statement is true: people don't care about what we know until they know that we care. As Christ brought the early Christians in "favour with all the people" (Acts 2:47), so also will He bring us into a positive relationship with those He wants us to share our faith with.

I have personally found that sharing God's Word with others plays a major role in Christians becoming strong in the Word, both in knowledge and in lifestyle. My favorite statement by Ellen White on the benefits of witnessing for Christ appears in the book *Steps to Christ*:

"If you will go to work as Christ designs that His disciples shall, and win souls for Him, you will feel the need of a deeper experience and a greater knowledge in divine things, and will hunger and thirst after righteousness. You will plead with God, and your faith will be strengthened, and your soul will drink deeper drafts at the well of salvation. Encountering opposition and trials will drive you to the Bible and prayer. You will grow in grace and the knowledge of Christ, and will develop a rich experience.

"The spirit of unselfish labor for others gives depth, stability, and Christlike loveliness to the character, and brings peace and happiness to its possessor. The aspirations are elevated. There is no room for sloth or selfishness. Those who thus exercise the Christian graces will grow and will become strong to work for God. They will have clear spiritual perceptions, a steady, growing faith, and an increased power in prayer. The Spirit of God, moving upon their spirit, calls forth the sacred harmonies of the soul in answer to the divine touch. Those who thus devote themselves to unselfish effort for the good of others are most surely working out their own salvation" (p. 80).

People ready to meet Jesus will be those who share Christ with others. Their witness for Christ will play an essential role in their victory over Satan. "And they overcame him by the blood of the Lamb, and by the word of their testimony; and they loved not their lives unto the death" (Rev. 12:11).

Personal Reflection and Discussion

1. What could we compare witnessing for Christ to in the physical world?

_____

_____

2. What will happen to our spiritual life if we neglect to witness?

_____

_____

3. List occasions you have found to be the best opportunities to witness.

_____

_____

4. What benefits do we receive when we share our faith with others?

_____

_____

_____

_____

Prayer Activity

- **Call your prayer partner and discuss this devotional with him/her.**
- **Pray with your prayer partner:**
    (1) for God to baptize you with His Holy Spirit.
    (2) for God to give you opportunities to witness for Him, and that you become more aware when they arise in your daily life.
    (3) for God to remove from you the fear of witnessing.
    (4) for the individuals on your prayer list.

Spiritual Fellowship

The Creation story teaches the need for fellowship. God made human beings to be very much like Himself: "God created man in his own image" (Gen. 1:27). The Lord intended human beings to be in perfect harmony or fellowship with Him and each other. All were to act together for their mutual benefit. That is why God said that "it is not good that the man should be alone" (Gen. 2:18). The Hebrew word translated "good" is *tov,* which means "pleasant, joyful or fruitful." What God is saying is that human beings would not achieve the joyfulness or fruitfulness that He intended if they were not in fellowship. In order for God's image to be manifest in the human race and for it to fulfill the purpose for which the Lord made it, humanity had to be a "fellowship," or community. The goal was that all humankind would be in perfect harmony, meeting each other's needs.

Christian fellowship is a central theme in the New Testament. In fact, the New Testament Greek word translated "fellowship" is *koinonia.* Its noun form means to share in, participate in, or to be actively involved in. The verb form means to communicate, distribute, and impart. In essence, *koinonia* involves ministering to one another. People share one another's hopes, dreams, struggles, and pains—all in a process of allowing God to use them to minister to others.

The early church experienced close fellowship with God and other believers. "And they continued stedfastly in the apostles' doctrine and fellowship, and in breaking of bread, and in prayers" (Acts 2:42).

God created human beings to desire others to share their deepest needs, struggles, hopes, and dreams with. Christian fellowship is where that is to happen. Paul referred to this when he declared: "Bear ye one another's burdens" (Gal. 6:2).

James also understood the vital importance of intimate fellowship among believers when he urged: "Confess your faults one to another, and pray one for another, that ye may be healed" (James 5:16). Sinful human beings are in a broken condition. Sin shatters humanity's fellowship with God and fellow beings. As the fruit of the Spirit and the gifts of the Spirit manifest themselves among Spirit-filled believers in a *koinonia* fellowship, great healing takes place. Such healing will affect the whole person—emotionally, spiritually, and physically.

Paul explained that a function of apostles, prophets, evangelists, pastors, and teachers in the church is "to prepare God's people for works of service, so that the body of Christ may be built up until we all reach unity in the faith and in the knowledge of the Son of God and become mature, attaining to the whole measure of the fullness of Christ. Then we will no longer be infants, tossed back and forth by the waves, and blown here and there by every wind of teaching and by the cunning and craftiness of men in their deceitful scheming. Instead, speaking the truth in love, we will in all things grow up into him who is the Head, that is, Christ. From him the whole body, joined and held together by every supporting ligament, grows and builds itself up in love, as each part does its work" (Eph. 4:12-16, NIV).

Here we find that close fellowship—Christians connecting with each other—is essential in order to attain "to the whole measure of the fullness of Christ." So it behooves every Christian to become part of a strong faith community. The home is usually the most conducive place for such fellowship to take place.

Christian fellowship is not only necessary for our personal spiritual growth—it also plays an important role in our emotional and physical health. Lester Breslow, former dean of the School of Public Health at UCLA, did a nine-year study of nearly 7,000 people in Alameda County in California. He discovered that individuals who had the most close friends had a 33 to 50 percent lower death rate than those with few close friends. Studies show that having even one close friend helps us to cope better with stress, a fact that plays an essential role in our emotional and physical health.

Personal Reflection and Discussion

1. Where does the Bible first present humanity's need for fellowship?

_____

_____

2. What does the New Testament Greek word translated "fellowship" mean?

_____

_____

3. What does James write that the Christian should do in order to experience healing?

_____

_____

4. What setting is best suited for *koinonia* fellowship to take place and why?

_____

_____

5. How do you think fellowship benefits one's spiritual, emotional, and physical health?

_____

_____

_____

_____

Prayer Activity

● **Call your prayer partner and discuss this devotional with him/her.**
● **Pray with your prayer partner:**
> **(1) for God to baptize you with His Holy Spirit.**
> **(2) for God to lead you into genuine Christian fellowship.**
> **(3) for the individuals on your prayer list.**

Diet and Spiritual Health

When we think of a healthy diet, we usually associate it with the body's physical health. It is certainly true that diet and physical health are linked together. However, diet also has a close connection to one's spiritual health.

Paul associated what one eats and drinks with spirituality when he wrote: "Whether therefore ye eat, or drink, or whatsoever ye do, do all to the glory of God" (1 Cor. 10:31). It is also the reason that God gave specific dietary instruction to His people in the Old Testament. He knew that food and drink would influence their relationship with Him.

Satan's first attack against humanity involved the area of appetite. Eve and then Adam both yielded to Satan's temptation. "And when the woman saw that the tree was good for food, and that it was pleasant to the eyes, and a tree to be desired to make one wise, she took of the fruit thereof, and did eat, and gave also unto her husband with her; and he did eat" (Gen. 3:6).

Ellen White many times in her writings emphasized the close relationship between diet and our spiritual strength.

"By the indulgence of perverted appetite, man loses his power to resist temptation" (*The Ministry of Healing,* p. 335).

Knowing this, Satan met Christ in the wilderness with a temptation associated with appetite. He remembered that he had been successful with the first Adam with such an approach, so he thought he would overcome Christ, the Second Adam, in the same manner.

"And Jesus being full of the Holy Ghost returned from Jordan, and was led by the Spirit into the wilderness, being forty days tempted of the devil. And in those days he did eat nothing: and when they were ended, he afterward hungered. And the devil said unto him, If thou be the Son of God, command this stone that it be made bread" (Luke 4:1-3).

Christ gained victory over appetite through faith in God's Word when He replied to Satan, "It is written, That man shall not live by bread alone, but by every word of God" (verse 4).

Unhealthy dietary practices will dull one's sense of right and wrong, weakening the defenses against Satan. The reason is that diet affects one's brain, the control room for all human action.

"The brain is the organ and instrument of the mind, and controls the whole body. In order for the other parts of the system to be healthy, the brain must be healthy. And in order for the brain to be healthy, the blood must be pure. If by correct habits of eating and drinking the blood is kept pure, the brain will be properly nourished" (*Medical Ministry,* p. 291).

Since God communicates with us through our brains, a healthy brain enables Him to do so more effectively. As a result, Satan has and is doing everything that he can to make our brains as unhealthy as possible. Ellen White very clearly explained this mechanism when she wrote:

"The brain nerves which communicate with the entire system are the only medium through which Heaven can communicate with man and affect his inmost life. Whatever disturbs the circulation of the electric currents in the nervous system lessens the strength of the vital powers, and the result is a deadening of the sensibilities of the mind" (*My Life Today,* p. 148).

Personal Reflection and Discussion

1. What instruction does the Bible give that indicates that diet and spirituality are closely linked?

_____

_____

2. In what area of humanity's being did Satan first attack Eve, Adam, and Christ?

_____

_____

3. What does an unhealthy diet do to our sense of right and wrong?

_____

_____

4. Describe how God communicates with the human race.

_____

_____

5. How does an unhealthy diet affect God's communication with us?

_____

_____

Prayer Activity

● Call your prayer partner and discuss this devotional with him/her.
● Pray with your prayer partner:
    (1) for God to baptize you with His Holy Spirit.
    (2) for God to lead you to learn what is a healthy diet and how to apply it to your life.
    (3) for the individuals on your prayer list.

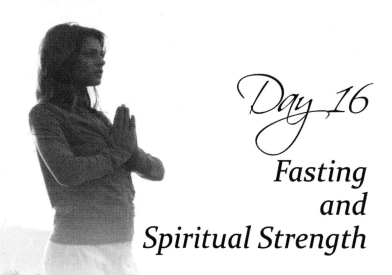

Fasting and Spiritual Strength

Fasting along with prayer will play an important role in preparing God's people to make it victoriously through the final crisis and be ready for Christ's second coming. Both increase the spiritual strength of God's people. Ellen White described it in the following way: "In order to succeed in such a conflict they must come to the work in a different spirit. Their faith must be strengthened by fervent *prayer and fasting*, and humiliation of heart. They must be emptied of self, and be filled with the Spirit and power of God. Earnest, persevering supplication to God in faith—faith that leads to entire dependence upon God, and unreserved consecration to His work—can alone avail to bring men the Holy Spirit's aid in the battle against principalities and powers, the rulers of the darkness of this world, and wicked spirits in high places" (*The Desire of Ages*, p. 431; italics supplied).

How does fasting and prayer spiritually strengthen us? Jesus connected strong faith with prayer and fasting. He stated that it was because of the disciples' "unbelief" that they were unable to cast out the devil when a father brought his child to the disciples for healing (Matt. 17:20). Then He added, "Howbeit this kind goeth not out but by prayer and fasting" (verse 21). Jesus made it very clear that prayer and fasting are an essential factor in strong faith. Thus if we want stronger faith to overcome Satan's influences in our life and ministry for the Lord, fasting and prayer must become a regular part of our Christian life.

Charles Finney was a spiritually powerful minister. He made the following statement about the results of personally receiving the baptism of the Holy Spirit, and the necessity of prayer and fasting in his ministry.

"I immediately found myself endued with such power from on high that a few words dropped here and there to individuals were the means of their immediate conversion. My words seemed to fasten like barbed arrows in the souls of men. They cut like a sword. They broke the heart like a hammer. Multitudes can attest to this. . . . Sometimes I would find myself . . . empty of this power. I would go and visit, and find that I made no saving impression. I would exhort and pray, with the same results. I would then set apart a day for private fasting and prayer. . . . After humbling myself, and crying out for help, the power would return upon me with all its freshness. This has been the experience of my life" (*The Praying Church Sourcebook*, p. 276).

Finney was not alone in his realization of the necessity of fasting and prayer in order to be strong in the Lord. Every outstanding leader of the Christian church throughout the centuries has understood the role that fasting plays in the advancement of God's work in one's life and ministry. Such prominent Christians as Polycarp, Tertulian, Martin Luther, John Calvin, John Knox, Jonathan Edwards, John Wesley, Charles Haddon Spurgeon, and Ellen White recognized this. The list could go on and on. Is it any wonder why Satan has tried to blind us to the truth about fasting! Fasting was so essential to John Wesley, founder of the Methodist Church, that he wrote: "The man that never fasts is no more in the way to heaven than the man who never prays"(*ibid.*, p. 291).

The spiritual benefits of fasting are numerous. It prompts us to prayer, thus enhancing our communion and fellowship with God. Such communion makes us more receptive to sense His leading in our lives, and better able to receive His instruction in a particular situation. That is why Christ fasted and prayed 40 days before beginning His ministry. Fasting opens our heart to God's direction in our life.

Personal Reflection and Discussion

1. What did Ellen White say about the necessity of fasting in the Christian's life and ministry?

_____

_____

2. What did Jesus say the lack of fasting caused in the disciples' ministry?

_____

_____

3. What did Jesus state was necessary for the disciples to have in order to experience the fullest power of God manifested in their life and ministry against Satan?

_____

_____

4. What does fasting do for the Christian?

_____

_____

Prayer Activity

● **Call your prayer partner and discuss this devotional with him/her.**
● **Pray with your prayer partner:**
    (1) for God to baptize you with His Holy Spirit.
    (2) for God to help you and your family to enter into a spiritual life that includes fasting and prayer.
    (3) for the individuals on your prayer list.

God's Natural Remedies

The God who created us is concerned about our well-being—physically, emotionally and spiritually. He has given counsel in His Word on how we can achieve good health. Both the Old Testament and New Testament offer such instruction.

The Bible contains experiences of God's children from the past. Paul tells us: "Now all these things happened unto them for ensamples: and they are written for our admonition, upon whom the ends of the world are come" (1 Cor. 10:11). We are to learn from them.

For example, Israel's deliverance out of Egypt is an important example for Christians living in the last days. The release of Israel from Egyptian bondage was a type of the deliverance of God's remnant people when Jesus comes the second time. Scripture tells us that there was not "one feeble person among their tribes" (Ps. 105:37). When Jesus returns, there will not be "one feeble" person among God's remnant. Why? Because they have learned and practiced the principles of health in every area of their lives. They will have attained by God's grace total health and healing.

God uses His natural laws of health to bring this about in our lives. Ellen White listed their basic categories as involving "pure air, sunlight, abstemiousness, rest, exercise, proper diet, the use of water, trust in divine power—these are the true remedies" (*The Ministry of Healing,* p. 127).

Understanding and following God's laws of health is vital if we desire to experience complete health in our life and be ready for Christ's second coming.

"In preparing a people for the Lord's second coming a great work is to be done through the promulgation of health principles. We are to relieve suffering by the use of the natural agencies that God has provided. We should teach the people how to prevent sickness by obedience to the laws of life, and while we work for the healing of the body we should seize every opportunity to work for the healing of the soul.

"This was Christ's method. He worked to restore both the physical and moral image of God in man. Both physical and moral health is to be communicated from the mighty Healer" (*Australasian Union Conference Record,* June 1, 1900).

Many research studies testify to the benefits of following the natural laws of health. We know today that many of the degenerative diseases, such as diabetes, heart disease, arthritis, etc., can be prevented. Several years ago a Long Beach Veterans Study followed 38 veterans ranging in age from 45 to 70. All suffered extensively from degenerative diseases. The researchers selected 19 as the experimental group and thoroughly examined them. For a full day they underwent X-ray, angiography, and four-color thermograph tests to determine the extent of artery damage from degenerative disease. Then the researchers put them on a low-fat, low-sugar, low-salt, and low-cholesterol diet with no caffeine. The group also followed an exercise regimen suitable for their age. The results were phenomenal. Within a matter of weeks their blood pressure dropped to normal, and blood cholesterol and blood triglyceride levels fell an average of 33 percent. Now they could walk miles without claudication or angina pain, which indicated their arteries were becoming unblocked. Most of the participants went off all the drugs they had been taking, walked several miles every day, and felt great.

Following God's laws of health is closely connected with our being able to glorify God in our life.

Spirituality and health are interrelated, a fact that Paul pointed out. "Whether therefore ye eat, or drink, or whatsoever ye do, do all to the glory of God" (1 Cor. 10:31). Ellen White declared that "the body is the only medium through which the mind and the soul are de- veloped for the upbuilding of character" (*The Ministry of Healing*, p. 130). Whatever adversely affects our physical health will negatively affect our spiritual health as well, and therefore could determine our eter- nal destiny.

Personal Reflection and Discussion

1. Why did God give health counsels in the Bible?

_____

_____

2. What was the condition of the Israelites when God led them out of Egypt?

_____

_____

3. What does the health of the Israelites when God delivered them out of Egypt say about His people when Jesus returns?

_____

_____

4. The "promulgation" of _____ _____ is to play an important role in "preparing a people for the Lord's second coming."

5. What are God's natural remedies?

_____

_____

6. What are some benefits of following God's natural remedies?

_____

_____

Prayer Activity

● **Call your prayer partner and discuss this devotional with him/her.**
● **Pray with your prayer partner:**
　(1) for God to baptize you with His Holy Spirit.
　(2) for God to lead you to apply His natural remedies in your life.
　(3) for the individuals on your prayer list.

Diet
and
Physical Health

We have known the relationship between a proper diet and physical health for some time. Every year more and more support comes from medical studies. As we have seen in previous devotional studies, following a healthy lifestyle, including a proper diet, is a matter of being a good steward of God, worshipping Him, and being His holy people.

The Bible informs the Christian about God's will in the area of diet by indicating which foods are clean, or acceptable to eat, and those that are unclean, or unacceptable for food. Since the principle every Christian should follow is to eat what is most healthful, many Christians as well as non-Christians are coming to the conclusion that a vegetarian diet is the healthiest.

Medical studies repeatedly show that a diet consisting primarily of fruits and vegetables is the best one to follow. A diet high in healthy carbohydrates such as fruits, vegetables, whole grains, and legumes can prevent many diseases. Study after study indicates that a diet composed of such foods will help prevent obesity, diabetes, high blood pressure, coronary heart disease, strokes, certain digestive problems, and some cancers.

The well-known Framingham Study followed 832 men for 20 years. For each grouping of three servings of fruits or vegetables per day there was a 45 percent decrease in the risk of death from stroke, as reported in the *Journal of the American Medical Association* (273, no. 14 [1995]: 1113-1117). Comparable benefits resulted for women who followed a similar diet.

A study of 764,343 adults reported by the National Cancer Institute found that a high-vegetable diet significantly reduced colon cancer. For men it reduced the risk by 25 percent and for women 40 percent. Numerous studies have demonstrated a close relationship between diet and cancer.

Such studies have shown that whole grains are much more beneficial than refined grains. The *American Journal of Clinical Nutrition* (70 [1999]: 412-419) reported in a 10-year study of 75,521 women that eating three or more servings a day of whole grains reduced their risk of coronary heart disease by 25 to 50 percent.

A 10-year Finland study of more than 4,300 men and women found that those who ate the most whole grains had a 35 percent less risk of type 2 diabetes. Those eating the highest amount of cereal fiber had 61 percent less risk.

The same beneficial relationship appears between whole-grain intake and the threat of stroke. In fact, an 11-year study of 15,792 individuals ages 45-64 found that those eating the most whole grains had a 48 percent decrease in death rates.

Such results do not just apply to adults. Children also have been found to benefit from diets high in fruits, vegetables, whole grains, and legumes.

God wants to influence the lives of men, women, and children. The diets we follow will play a significant role in His being able to carry out His will in our lives. Therefore, especially as we near Christ's second coming, we need to consider seriously the kind of foods that we consume. Remember what Ellen White wrote:

"The body is the only medium through which the mind and the soul are developed for the upbuilding of character" (*The Ministry of Healing,* p. 130).

She also informed us of the best diet to follow:

"Grains, fruits, nuts, and vegetables constitute the diet chosen for us by our Creator. These foods, prepared in as simple and natural a manner as possible, are the most healthful and nourishing. They impart a strength, a power of endurance, and a vigor of intellect, that are not afforded by a more complex and stimulating diet" (*Counsels on Diet and Foods,* p. 81). As we approach Christ's return it is essential that we have the "strength, endurance, and vigor of intellect" that Ellen White said such foods will provide.

Personal Reflection and Discussion

1. In what two categories does the Bible classify food?

_____

_____

2. What kind of diet are both Christians and non-Christians finding to be most healthy?

_____

_____

3. What does a healthy diet consist of?

_____

_____

4. List some of the benefits of following a vegetarian diet.

_____

_____

_____

5. Why is a healthy diet important for a Christian as we near Christ's second coming?

_____

_____

6. What did Ellen White say about our bodies and developing Christ's character?

_____

_____

Prayer Activity

- **Call your prayer partner and discuss this devotional with him/her.**
- **Pray with your prayer partner:**
    - **(1) for God to baptize you with His Holy Spirit.**
    - **(2) for God to help you be motivated to honor Him by consistently following a healthy diet.**
    - **(3) for the individuals on your prayer list.**

A Far-reaching Decision

The book of Daniel is unique in the Bible in that it gives both stories and important prophecies for God's children to understand throughout the ages. It especially has lessons and prophetic insights necessary for those living in the last days.

Each story in Daniel gives us insights into the experiences that God's people will go through at the end of time. The book begins with the story of Nebuchadnezzar selecting Daniel and his three friends, Hananiah, Mishael, and Azariah, to be educated and groomed to become leaders in the Babylonian Empire. It was a great honor for Daniel and his friends.

The king, of course, wanted them to have the very best food and drink in order to be healthy, and develop into the leaders he wanted them to become. However, the problem was that what the king considered healthy food and drink did not agree with what God had revealed to Daniel and his friends. They immediately faced a serious decision. Should they consider it an honor to have been chosen by the king for leadership roles in Babylon and go along with eating the food the king had provided? After all, refusing to eat the king's food was a sign of political disloyalty in the biblical world and could lead to their deaths. It would prevent them from becoming leaders in the nation of Babylon and using their influence for God. So from a human perspective they had many good reasons to abide by the king's orders, and partake of the food and drink that he had provided.

However, Daniel and his three friends knew it was never safe to follow human wisdom instead of God's clear instruction in His Word. Therefore, "Daniel purposed in his heart that he would not defile himself with the portion of the king's meat, nor with the wine which he drank: therefore he requested of the prince of the eunuchs that he might not defile himself" (Dan. 1:8).

The Lord had prepared the way for him to make his request. "God had brought Daniel into favour and tender love with the prince of the eunuchs" (verse 9). But even though the leader of the eunuchs wanted to meet Daniel's request, he was afraid that the king would be angry with him for switching the food. So Daniel proposed a test and told the official: "Prove thy servants, I beseech thee, ten days; and let them give us pulse to eat, and water to drink. Then let our countenances be looked upon before thee, and the countenance of the children that eat of the portion of the king's meat: and as thou seest, deal with thy servants" (verses 12, 13). The official agreed, and God blessed their diet of vegetables and water. "And at the end of ten days their countenances appeared fairer and fatter in flesh than all the children which did eat the portion of the king's meat" (verse 15).

As a result of Daniel and his friends remaining faithful to God's health principles the Lord was able to bless them abundantly. "As for these four children, God gave them knowledge and skill in all learning and wisdom: and Daniel had understanding in all visions and dreams" (verse 17). When the king asked that they be brought before him, their mental ability amazed him. "And in all matters of wisdom and understanding, that the king enquired of them, he found them ten times better than all the magicians and astrologers that were in all his realm" (verse 20).

Their faithfulness to God in the area of healthful

living was essential for God to be able to carry out His plan in their lives. Here we see that following His health laws prepared the way for the "rest of the story" in Daniel—stories of victory after victory. It also teaches us the importance that health principles will play in the lives of God's last-day people as they go victoriously through earth's final crisis and become ready for Christ's second coming.

Personal Reflection and Discussion

1. In what honored position did King Nebuchadnezzar place Daniel and his three friends?

_____
_____

2. What did the king provide for them in order for them to develop into the leaders he wanted them to become?

_____
_____

3. What did Daniel and his friends do when asked to eat the king's food and drink his wine?

_____
_____

4. What was the result of their faithfulness to God?

_____
_____

5. How do you think this story applies to God's last-day people?

_____
_____

Prayer Activity

- Call your prayer partner and discuss this devotional with him/her.
- Pray with your prayer partner:
    (1) for God to open your understanding as you study your daily devotional.
    (2) for God to lead you to grasp and apply His dietary health principles in your life.
    (3) for the individuals on your prayer list.

Day 20

Exercise and Physical Health

God, knowing humanity's need of exercise, put Adam "into the Garden of Eden to dress it and to keep it" (Gen. 2:15). Today exercise is becoming more and more recognized as a vital component to achieving good physical health. Yet Ellen White understood this many years ago when she wrote:

"The time spent in physical exercise is not lost. . . . A proportionate exercise of all the organs and faculties of the body is essential to the best work of each. When the brain is constantly taxed while the other organs of the living machinery are inactive, there is a loss of strength, physical and mental. The physical system is robbed of its healthful tone, the mind loses its freshness and vigor, and a morbid excitability is the result" (*The Adventist Home,* p. 494).

She also noted the importance of children getting enough exercise.

"Children and youth who are kept at school and confined to books cannot have sound physical constitutions. The exercise of the brain in study, without corresponding physical exercise, has a tendency to attract the blood to the brain, and the circulation of the blood through the system becomes unbalanced. The brain has too much blood, and the extremities too little. There should be rules regulating the studies of children and youth to certain hours, and then a portion of their time should be spent in physical labor" (*Child Guidance,* p. 340).

The *Journal of the American Medical Association* (273, no. 5 [1995]: 402-407) reports that regular physical exercise reduces the risk of obesity, high blood pressure, heart disease and stroke, diabetes, osteoporosis, many cancers, and anxiety and depression. The same journal also reports the amazing statistic that smokers who exercise regularly have a lower risk of dying from a heart attack than nonsmokers who do not exercise. Estimates are that in the United States 250,000 deaths a year result from a lack of regular physical exercise. Studies show that of all lifestyle factors for good health, exercise is the number one factor.

A study of 25,892 men ages 30-87 reported in *Sports and Exercise Fitness* (34, no. 5 [2002]: 735-739) indicated that the fit individuals had a 55 percent lower risk of dying from cancer than the less-fit person. Physical fitness through physical exercise has a close relationship to cancer mortality. Studies have shown the same benefit for women. Women 50 and older who exercise regularly have 67 percent less breast cancer (*Cancer Epidemiology, Biomarkers, and Prevention* 10 [July 2001]: 809, 810).

An example of the benefits of exercise is the case of a woman in her 80s named Eula Weaver. A great-grandmother on many drugs for arthritis and atherosclerosis symptoms (angina and high blood pressure), she could walk only 50 feet. Physicians put her on a strict diet and exercise program. After six months she could go several city blocks at one outing. Within two years, at age 86, she was jogging more than one mile per day and was off all drugs. After three years she entered the summer Senior Olympics in Irvine, California, and won gold medals in the half-mile and one-mile run (*Journal of the American Medical Association* 229 [1974]: 1266, 1267).

Ellen White also emphasized similar benefits. "Walking, in all cases where it is possible, is the best remedy for diseased bodies, because in this exercise all the organs of the body are brought into use. Many who depend upon the movement cure could accomplish more for themselves by muscular exercise than the movements can do for them. In some cases want of exercise causes the bowels and muscles to become enfeebled and shrunken, and these organs that have become enfeebled for want of use will be strengthened by exercise. There is no exercise that can take the place of walking. By it the circulation of the blood is greatly improved" (*Testimonies for the Church,* vol. 3, p. 78).

God holds us accountable for the use and care of our physical abilities and health. Following good health practices is a moral issue.

"The misuse of our physical powers shortens the period of time in which our lives can be used for the glory of God. And it unfits us to accomplish the work God has given us to do. By allowing ourselves to form wrong habits, by keeping late hours, by gratifying appetite at the expense of health, we lay the foundation for feebleness. By neglecting physical exercise, by overworking mind or body, we unbalance the nervous system. Those who thus shorten their lives and unfit themselves for service by disregarding nature's laws are guilty of robbery toward God" (*Christ's Object Lessons,* p. 346).

Personal Reflection and Discussion

1. What did Ellen White say about the importance of physical exercise?

_____

_____

2. Why is physical exercise also fundamental for children?

_____

_____

3. List some of the medically proven benefits of regular physical exercise.

_____

_____

4. Why is neglecting to exercise regularly a moral issue?

_____

_____

5. What do you think is the best regular physical exercise for you?

_____

_____

Prayer Activity

- Call your prayer partner and discuss this devotional with him/her.
- Pray with your prayer partner:
    (1) for God to baptize you with His Holy Spirit.
    (2) for God to help you develop a regular habit of physical exercise.
    (3) for the individuals on your prayer list.

Water and Physical Health

Water is fundamental to life. It is so essential that Christ used it to illustrate the gift of eternal life that He has to offer: "But whosoever drinketh of the water that I shall give him shall never thirst; but the water that I shall give him shall be in him a well of water springing up into everlasting life" (John 4:14). The body consists of about 60 percent water. The brain's ratio of water is even greater. Thus it should be clear that our water intake is vital in order to keep the amount in the body at a healthy level. Ellen White wrote concerning the importance of drinking water:

"In health and in sickness, pure water is one of Heaven's choicest blessings. Its proper use promotes health. It is the beverage which God provided to quench the thirst of animals and man. Drunk freely, it helps to supply the necessities of the system, and assists nature to resist disease" (*Counsels on Diet and Foods,* p. 419).

Water is necessary for the body's cells and organs to function properly. Because many nutrients are water soluble, it plays a crucial role in their assimilation. In addition, water helps maintain proper blood viscosity so this life-giving fluid can flow freely in the body, bringing the needed nutrients to every cell and organ. Also, low levels of water make it more difficult for the body to eliminate toxins and waste products. Their buildup will create an unhealthy environment within the body. Because of this, if the water level falls below a healthy level, it puts extra strain on the heart, lungs, and kidneys, and can even cause damage.

Body metabolism—the processes in the body necessary for life—creates heat. That is why, for example, we get hot when we exercise. Water is essential for dissipating such heat. If the heat does not get removed, body organs will become hotter than the normal range for their healthy function, possibly damaging them. As a result, overheating and heatstroke are extremely serious. If the water level falls too low in the body, it will not have enough to allow cooling, and death can occur. The body cools by evaporation of water from the pores of the skin. A proper level of water is necessary for it to take place properly.

Physicians recommend six to eight eight-ounce glasses of water a day in order to maintain proper water levels in the body. One cannot depend on thirst to remind us to drink water. We should schedule regular water drinking throughout the day. For example, drinking a glass of water upon rising in the morning, a glass of water a half hour before each meal, and a glass of water midway between each meal would result in six glasses of water a day. Ellen White gave practical instruction on when to drink water.

"Many make a mistake in drinking cold water with their meals. Taken with meals, water diminishes the flow of the salivary glands; and the colder the water, the greater the injury to the stomach. . . . To quench thirst, pure water drank some little time before or after the meal is all that nature requires" (*Review and Herald,* July 29, 1884).

The proper use of water outside the body is also conducive to good health. It benefits us in many ways.

"Whether a person is sick or well, respiration is more free and easy if bathing is practiced. By it the muscles become more flexible, the mind and body are alike invigorated, the intellect is made brighter, and every faculty becomes livelier. The bath is a soother of the nerves. It promotes general perspiration, quickens the circulation, overcomes obstructions in the system, and acts beneficially on the kidneys and urinary organs. Bathing helps the bowels, stomach, and liver, giving energy and new life to each. It also promotes digestion, and instead of the system being weakened, it is strengthened. Instead of increasing the liability to cold, a bath, properly taken, fortifies against cold because the circulation is improved and the uterine organs, which are more or less congested, are relieved; for the blood is brought to the surface, and a more easy and regular flow of the blood through all the blood vessels is obtained" (*Testimonies for the Church,* vol. 3, pp. 70, 71).

Personal Reflection and Discussion

1. What percent of the body consists of water?

_____

_____

2. List some of the medically proven benefits of drinking water.

_____

_____

3. Why should we not drink water with our meals?

_____

_____

4. List a schedule for drinking an eight-ounce glass of water in order to consume six glasses a day.

_____

_____

5. List some of the benefits of bathing in water?

_____

_____

Prayer Activity

● **Call your prayer partner and discuss this devotional with him/her.**
● **Pray with your prayer partner:**
    (1) for God to baptize you with His Holy Spirit.
    (2) for God to help you to remember to drink enough water each day.
    (3) for the individuals on your prayer list.

Day 22

Sunlight, Fresh Air, and Physical Health

We often take sunlight and fresh air for granted. However, they are two means that God uses to bless His living creation—plants, animals, and humanity. In order for us to have optimal health, it is essential that we get enough sunlight and fresh air. Ellen White recognized this when she wrote:

"And when I violate the laws God has established in my being, I am to repent and reform, and place myself in the most favorable condition under the doctors God has provided—pure air, pure water, and the healing, precious sunlight" (*Child Guidance,* p. 367).

"Exercise, and a free, abundant use of the air and sunlight—blessings which Heaven has bestowed upon all—would in many cases give life and strength to the emaciated invalid" (*Christian Temperance and Bible Hygiene,* p. 160).

"I must get all the sunlight that it is possible for me to obtain. I must have wisdom to be a faithful guardian of my body" (*Counsels on Diet and Foods,* p. 302).

"By such employment and the free use of air and sunlight, many an emaciated invalid might recover health and strength" (*The Ministry of Healing,* p. 246).

Research today has revealed the contributions of sunlight and fresh air to good health. Sunlight plays an essential role in getting full nutrition from the food we eat. It also assists in the prevention of such ailments as seasonal affective disorder (SAD), osteoporosis, type 2 diabetes, and even some cancers.

One of the major roles of sunlight is that it provides the vitamin D necessary for absorption of calcium for bone strength. Vitamin D also increases the production of endorphins, which function in our brain to maintain a healthy nervous system. It even assists in lowering the cholesterol level in the blood. Research has linked vitamin D deficiency to such autoimmune diseases as Crohn's disease, multiple sclerosis, rheumatoid arthritis, and thyroditis.

In addition, sunlight destroys bacteria, viruses, and mold that can cause infections. Proper amounts of sunlight will increase the white blood cell count, and it also improves the ability of red blood cells to carry oxygen.

Fresh air is as essential as sunlight for good health. It cleans our lungs of impurities that we breathe into our body every day. Deep breaths of fresh air provide us with the much-needed oxygen so that our body's cells can function effectively. It gives us more energy and makes our brains more alert and clear (which by the way consumes 20 percent of the oxygen we breathe in). If we want to have clarity of mind in order to better commune with God and have clear spiritual discernment, we must get enough oxygen into our system.

When we consider all these facts, we begin to see the essential role that exercise in the open air and exposure to sunlight play in our physical as well as our spiritual health. Once again we recognize that because God created us as multidimensional beings, what affects one dimension will ultimately have an impact on the others. Poor health habits will disturb our physical, emotional, and spiritual well-being.

Personal Reflection and Discussion

1. What did Ellen White list as benefits of sunlight and fresh air?

_____

_____

2. List some of the medically proven physical benefits of sunlight.

_____

_____

3. List some of the medically proven physical contributions of fresh air.

_____

_____

4. What do sunlight and fresh air have to do with our emotional well-being?

_____

_____

5. What do sunlight and fresh air have to do with our spiritual well-being?

_____

_____

Prayer Activity

- **Call your prayer partner and discuss this devotional with him/her.**
- **Pray with your prayer partner:**
  - **(1) for God to baptize you with His Holy Spirit.**
  - **(2) for God to help you get enough sunlight and fresh air every day in order to have good physical, emotional, and spiritual health.**
  - **(3) for the individuals on your prayer list.**

Rest and Physical Health

Jesus knew the importance of rest when he told His disciples, "Come ye yourselves apart into a desert place, and rest a while" (Mark 6:31). For there were many coming and going, and they had no leisure so much as to eat" (verse 31). Christ realized that continuous work even for the Lord, without time to recuperate, would be harmful to Himself and His disciples. They needed the physical, emotional, and spiritual benefits that such rest provided, a fact that Ellen White understood as well.

"The importance of regularity in the time for eating and sleeping should not be overlooked. Since the work of building up the body takes place during the hours of rest, it is essential, especially in youth, that sleep should be regular and abundant" (*Education*, p. 205).

The lives of most Christians are filled with family, work, commuting, children, church activities—the list could go on and on. They have little time to slow down and rest. Our hectic schedules not only interfere with times of rest during the day, but even infringe on our getting the needed sleep at night. Such practices make us less capable of dealing with the numerous daily stresses of life. Not getting enough rest will adversely affect our mental and physical health, which will wreak havoc with our spiritual well-being.

Proper rest cycles during intense physical activity will enhance the benefits of the physical exercise. A physical exercise regimen requires rest between workouts to allow the muscles, tendons, and ligaments to heal from the strain put on them. If such rest does not happen, extensive damage to the body can take place. On the other hand, the muscles strengthen during the time of rest following exercise.

Psychology professor James B. Maas of Cornell University has shown in his research that we need eight hours of sleep each night. If we do not get that amount of rest, it will impair our alertness, productivity, and creativity, negatively affecting our general health. The reason that getting enough hours of sleep each night is essential is that REM (rapid eye movement) sleep takes place between the seventh and eighth hour of sleep. It is the time that the brain repairs itself and grows new connections. Surveys indicate that one third of all Americans get only six hours of sleep a night or less.

Clinical research shows that getting enough rest at night as well as relaxation during the day provides many physical benefits to our body. It reduces stress hormones, strengthens our immune system (thus making us more resistant to disease), and lowers blood pressure and cholesterol.

A study presented at the Associated Professional Sleep Societies, in Seattle, Washington, involved 62 children and categorized them as either napping (77 percent) or nonnapping (23 percent). The researchers found that those who didn't take daytime naps had higher levels of anxiety, hyperactivity, and depression. In a news release Brian Crosby, a postdoctoral fellow of Pennsylvania State University, said: "There is a lot of individual variability in [the age] when children are ready to give up naps. I would encourage parents to include a quiet 'rest' time in their daily schedule that would allow children to nap if necessary."

Satan certainly knows the important role that rest plays in our physical, emotional, and spiritual well-being. No wonder he has worked so hard to lead our society to become more and more sleep-deprived without any time to relax during the day. He is even attacking our children in this area. More and more studies show how few hours of sleep per night teenagers and college students get. If we want to experience optimal physical, emotional, and spiritual health, we must see that we and our family get enough rest.

Personal Reflection and Discussion

1. What did Ellen White say the benefits of rest were?

_____

_____

2. List some of the medically proven physical benefits of rest.

_____

_____

3. List some of the medically proven emotional contributions of rest.

_____

_____

4. What do you think rest has to do with our spiritual well-being?

_____

_____

Prayer Activity

- **Call your prayer partner and discuss this devotional with him/her.**
- **List some of the medically proven emotional contributions of rest. Pray with your prayer partner:**
    (1) for God to baptize you with His Holy Spirit.
    (2) for God to help you and your family to get enough rest every day in order to have good physical, emotional, and spiritual health.
    (3) for the individuals on your prayer list.

At the conclusion of His work of creation God rested and established the seventh day as a rest day for all His creation. "Thus the heavens and the earth were finished, and all the host of them. And on the seventh day God ended his work which he had made; and he rested on the seventh day from all his work which he had made. And God blessed the seventh day, and sanctified it: because that in it he had rested from all his work which God created and made" (Gen. 2:1-3).

God did not rest because He was tired. Rather, He ceased His work of creation in part to begin communion with the man, Adam, that He had created to have dominion in the Garden of Eden prepared especially for him. God knew that human beings would need the seventh-day rest in order to maintain the relationship that He desired to have with them. God reemphasized the importance of the seventh day of rest when He gave Moses the Ten Commandments.

"Remember the sabbath day, to keep it holy. Six days shalt thou labour, and do all thy work: But the seventh day is the sabbath of the Lord thy God: in it thou shalt not do any work, thou, nor thy son, nor thy daughter, thy manservant, nor thy maidservant, nor thy cattle, nor thy stranger that is within thy gates: For in six days the Lord made heaven and earth, the sea, and all that in them is, and rested the seventh day: wherefore the Lord blessed the sabbath day, and hallowed it" (Ex. 20:8-11).

After sin entered the world human beings not only needed to observe the seventh-day Sabbath for spiritual strengthening with God but also for physical and emotional health. As we saw in yesterday's devotional, rest is essential to our total well-being. God is so concerned about it that He has given us specific instruction on how to get the greatest blessing from the Sabbath rest.

"If thou turn away thy foot from the sabbath, from doing thy pleasure on my holy day; and call the sabbath a delight, the holy of the Lord, honourable; and shalt honour him, not doing thine own ways, nor finding thine own pleasure, nor speaking thine own words: Then shalt thou delight thyself in the Lord; and I will cause thee to ride upon the high places of the earth, and feed thee with the heritage of Jacob thy father: for the mouth of the Lord hath spoken it" (Isa. 58:13, 14).

Our Creator knew that simply ceasing from physical labor was not enough. In order for His children to receive the greatest benefit, He asks us even to stop thinking about what concerns us during the other days of the week. That is why He says that we are not to even speak our own words. Life is stressful, and we need a break from its concerns. When we follow God's instruction to rest our minds from the cares of life and our bodies from physical work, and focus on Him, we will receive not only spiritual strengthening but also emotional and physical benefits.

Furthermore, God's command for us to rest from our labors every seventh-day Sabbath is a type of our rest in Him for our redemption. The Sabbath rest is symbolic of resting completely in Christ for our deliverance from temptation and sin. The Old Testament tells us that the Sabbath commemorates two things. It is a memorial of God's creating the earth and all that is in it (Ex. 20:8-11), and also of God's redemptive work in our lives. "Moreover also I gave them my sabbaths, to be a sign between me and them, that they might know that I am the Lord that sanctify them" (Eze. 20:12).

Every week when we rest on the seventh-day Sabbath we are celebrating God's work of redemption in our life. However, if we have not entered the rest of redemption by accepting by faith what God has done for us, we are not truly entering into the deeper spiritual meaning of Sabbath rest. If we are seeking to obey God through our own efforts, not trusting fully in Christ to do the work, we fail to experience the Sabbath rest that God intends us to experience and extol. The true resting in Christ for our salvation will benefit us not only spiritually but also emotionally and physically.

Personal Reflection and Discussion

1. What did God do on the seventh day after Creation?

_____

_____

2. Why did God rest on the seventh day?

_____

_____

3. Why did God give Adam the seventh-day Sabbath?

_____

_____

4. After sin entered the world, what benefit did the seventh-day Sabbath provide for God's children?

_____

_____

5. Why does God ask us not even to speak our own words on the Sabbath?

_____

_____

6. What does the seventh-day Sabbath rest symbolize concerning our relationship with Christ?

_____

_____

Prayer Activity

● **Call your prayer partner and discuss this devotional with him/her.**
● **Pray with your prayer partner:**
 (1) for God to baptize you with His Holy Spirit.
 (2) for God to help you understand and experience the full benefits of Sabbath rest.
 (3) for the individuals on your prayer list.

Alcohol and Physical Health

The Bible is clear about the dangers of alcohol. "Wine is a mocker, strong drink is raging: and whosoever is deceived thereby is not wise" (Prov. 20:1).

"Who hath woe? who hath sorrow? who hath contentions? who hath babbling? who hath wounds without cause? who hath redness of eyes? They that tarry long at the wine; they that go to seek mixed wine. Look not thou upon the wine when it is red, when it giveth his colour in the cup, when it moveth itself aright. At the last it biteth like a serpent, and stingeth like an adder. Thine eyes shall behold strange women, and thine heart shall utter perverse things. Yea, thou shalt be as he that lieth down in the midst of the sea, or as he that lieth upon the top of a mast. They have stricken me, shalt thou say, and I was not sick; they have beaten me, and I felt it not: when shall I awake? I will seek it yet again" (Prov. 23:29-35).

Ellen White strongly advocated Scripture's view of the dangers of alcohol. She clearly pointed out the threat it and other stimulants pose to one's spirituality.

" 'Abstain from fleshly lusts, which war against the soul' (1 Peter 2:11), is the language of the apostle Peter. Many regard this warning as applicable only to the licentious; but it has a broader meaning. It guards against every injurious gratification of appetite or passion. It is a most forcible warning against the use of such stimulants and narcotics as tea, coffee, tobacco, alcohol, and morphine. These indulgences may well be classed among the lusts that exert a pernicious influence upon moral character. The earlier these hurtful habits are formed, the more firmly will they hold their victims in slavery to lust, and the more certainly will they lower the standard of spirituality" (*Counsels on Health,* pp. 67, 68).

"When they are under the influence of the liquid poison, they are in Satan's control. He rules them, and they cooperate with him" (*Temperance,* p. 24).

Medical science has linked alcohol to such physical problems as poor physical coordination, reduced mental alertness, and diminished decision-making ability—all of which pose a danger to oneself and others. Some estimate that alcohol consumption lurks behind almost half of all physical injuries.

In addition, alcohol use also leads to some serious long-term physical health problems, ranging from a higher risk for heart disease, liver disease, circulatory problems, peptic ulcers, various forms of cancer, to even irreversible brain damage. Other health problems caused by alcohol include damage to the pancreas and the kidneys. Alcohol consumption can cause malnutrition by disrupting the absorption of nutrients in food. It can also lead to suppression of the immune system, which increases the potential for all kinds of illness. Researchers estimate that alcohol yearly attributes to $15 billion in health-care costs, which calculates to 12 percent of adult health-care expenses.

Statistics show that alcohol contributes to 100,000 deaths in the United States annually, which ranks third in the leading causes of preventable deaths in the U.S. Tobacco and diet-related deaths are the only two that rank higher than alcohol in preventable deaths.

Alcohol drinking is dangerous for pregnant women. It increases the risk of low-birth-weight babies and intrauterine growth retardation, which magnifies the danger of infection and long-term developmental problems.

The evidence is irrefutable. Alcohol is a dangerous drug. Those who use it are putting themselves at risk of physical illness and emotional problems as well as weakening their spiritual perceptions and relationship with God. Anyone preparing for Christ's soon return will not want to drink alcohol in any form.

You will note that Ellen White listed tea and coffee along with tobacco, alcohol, and morphine. One of the objectionable components of tea, coffee, and cola drinks is caffeine. Caffeine is in the same family of drugs as nicotine and morphine. The *Journal of Bone and Mineral Research* stated in 2009 that caffeine increases the risk of osteoporosis in elderly women. According to hypertension specialist Sheldon Sheps, M.D., of the Mayo Clinic, it is known to cause blood pressure spikes. Professor Roland Griffiths, of Johns Hopkins School of Medicine, points out that caffeine is an addictive drug and can cause withdrawl symptoms when one tries to stop injecting it. Medical studies continue to support the importance of avoiding such drugs as nicotine and caffeine.

Personal Reflection and Discussion

1. What does the Bible say about the dangers of using alcohol?

_____
_____

2. What did Ellen White warn about alcohol?

_____
_____

3. List some of the medically proven dangers from alcohol.

_____
_____

4. Why would those preparing for Christ's second coming not use alcohol?

_____
_____

5. How does using alcohol affect one's relationship with God?

_____
_____

Prayer Activity

● Call your prayer partner and discuss this devotional with him/her.
● Pray with your prayer partner:
    (1) for God to baptize you with His Holy Spirit.
    (2) for God to help you and your family to abstain from the use of alcohol in order to achieve the relationship with Him that He wants you to have.
    (3) for the individuals on your prayer list.

Tobacco and Physical Health

The Bible instructs us: "I beseech you therefore, brethren, by the mercies of God, that ye present your bodies a living sacrifice, holy, acceptable unto God, which is your reasonable service. And be not conformed to this world: but be ye transformed by the renewing of your mind, that ye may prove what is that good, and acceptable, and perfect, will of God" (Rom. 12:1, 2).

This means that we are to allow no practice in our life that will have a negative impact on our health, whether it be physically, emotionally, or spiritually. Scripture does not have specific counsel about tobacco, since it was not an issue during biblical times. However, the principle of presenting our bodies as healthy as possible to God covers anything detrimental to our health, which certainly includes the use of tobacco. Ellen White took a strong position against it.

"Tobacco is a slow, insidious poison, and its effects are more difficult to cleanse from the system than those of liquor" (*Testimonies for the church,* vol. 3, p. 569).

In the same book she stated, "Tobacco using is a habit which frequently affects the nervous system in a more powerful manner than does the use of alcohol. It binds the victim in stronger bands of slavery than does the intoxicating cup; the habit is more difficult to overcome. Body and mind are, in many cases, more thoroughly intoxicated with the use of tobacco than with spirituous liquors, for it is a more subtle poison" (p. 562).

She pointed out that it adversely affects one's relationship with God. "Tobacco, in whatever form it is used, tells upon the constitution. It is a slow poison. It affects the brain and benumbs the sensibilities, so that

the mind cannot clearly discern spiritual things, especially those truths which would have a tendency to correct this filthy indulgence. Those who use tobacco in any form are not clear before God. In such a filthy practice it is impossible for them to glorify God in their bodies and spirits which are His. And while they are using slow and sure poisons, which are ruining their health and debasing the faculties of the mind, God cannot approbate them. He may be merciful to them while they indulge in this pernicious habit in ignorance of the injury it is doing them, but when the matter is set before them in its true light, then they are guilty before God if they continue to indulge this gross appetite" (*Counsels on Health,* p. 81).

She even indicated that tobacco weakens the body's ability to heal.

"God's healing power runs all through nature. If a human being cuts his flesh or breaks a bone, nature at once begins to heal the injury, and thus preserve the man's life. But man can place himself in a position where nature is trammeled so that she cannot do her work. . . . If tobacco is used, . . . the healing power of nature is weakened to a greater or less extent" (*Medical Ministry,* p. 11).

Medical science could not be more clear about the dangers of tobacco. It raises the risk of cancer, high blood pressure, strokes, and heart disease. Inhaling tobacco smoke causes lung cancer, sinus disease, and chronic obstructive lung disease. Many pipe smokers assume that their smoking is less harmful. However, research shows that they have an increased chance of lung, larynx, throat, esophagus, pancreas, and colorectal cancers. They also face a greater possibility of coronary artery disease, emphysema, chronic bronchitis, and strokes.

For every eight days an individual smokes he or she loses one day of life. But quitting smoking at any age brings health benefits. Studies show that those who stop before age 50 cut their risk of dying during the next 15 years by 50 percent.

The facts are clear. Tobacco use is a serious danger to anyone's physical health. Ellen White reminded us that it adversely imperils our relationship with God by its effects on our mind. Our mind is the means that He employs to communicate with us and to influence our behavior. Therefore, those ready for Christ's return will not touch tobacco, because they know its use will make them unprepared to have the relationship with God necessary to be victorious through the final crisis and to stand in the presence of Christ in all His glory when He returns.

Personal Reflection and Discussion

1. What did Ellen White say about the use of tobacco?

_____

_____

2. What teaching in the Bible would lead a Christian to choose not to use tobacco?

_____

_____

3. List some of the medically proven dangers in using tobacco.

_____

_____

4. Why would those preparing for Christ's second coming not employ tobacco?

_____

_____

5. How does using tobacco affect one's relationship with God?

_____

_____

Prayer Activity

- Call your prayer partner and discuss this devotional with him/her.
- Pray with your prayer partner:
    (1) for God to baptize you with His Holy Spirit.
    (2) for God to help you and your family to abstain from the use of tobacco in order to achieve the relationship with God that He wants you to have with Him.
    (3) for the individuals on your prayer list.

Temperance and Physical Health

In order to achieve optimal health of body, mind, and spirit we must practice temperance is every aspect of our lifestyle. Paul instructed us that "every man that striveth for the mastery is temperate in all things. Now they do it to obtain a corruptible crown; but we an incorruptible. I therefore so run, not as uncertainly; so fight I, not as one that beateth the air: But I keep under my body, and bring it into subjection: lest that by any means, when I have preached to others, I myself should be a castaway" (1 Cor. 9:25-27).

One of the qualities that the Holy Spirit will strive to bring into our life when we seek to be filled with His presence is temperance: "But the fruit of the Spirit is love, joy, peace, longsuffering, gentleness, goodness, faith, meekness, *temperance*: against such there is no law" (Gal. 5:22, 23).

Ellen White clearly instructed us concerning the relationship between temperance and the sanctified experience in Christ.

"God's people are to learn the meaning of temperance in all things. . . . All self-indulgence is to be cut away from their lives. Before they can really understand the meaning of true sanctification and of conformity to the will of Christ, they must, by cooperating with God, obtain the mastery over wrong habits and practices" (*Child Guidance,* p. 396).

Temperance means more than just abstaining from alcohol, tobacco, and other harmful drugs. It calls for moderation in all things—eating, drinking, working, mental exertion, etc. How we practice temperance will determine to what extent we reveal God's glory in our life, which is His character.

"Whether therefore ye eat, or drink, or whatsoever ye do, do all to the glory of God" (1 Cor. 10:31).

Thus we must practice temperance in all things in order to attain the most healthful condition of our every faculty. Those who have sedentary jobs would do well to eat less than those who have physically active occupations. Overeating will cause weight gain and lead to many health problems, such as high blood pressure, high cholesterol, heart disease, diabetes—the list could go on and on. Someone who eats too little will also encounter severe health issues. Extreme cases of being underweight can lead to death, as we see in cases of anorexia and bulimia. The body's organs don't get enough nutrition and will eventually cease to function.

Medical science has shown that exercise is perhaps the most important factor in achieving good health. Yet even that can be harmful if carried to excess. Too much exercise can damage tendons, ligaments, bones, cartilage, and joints. If continued, minor injuries will not have a chance to heal, which can result in long-term damage.

Sunlight is essential to health. However, we have known for some time that prolonged exposure to it can cause the skin to lose its elasticity or develop cancer.

Every one of the natural remedies that the Lord has given us (diet, exercise, sunlight, rest, etc.) can be misused in ways that will have a negative impact on us physically, emotionally, and spiritually if we do not employ temperance in them.

Personal Reflection and Discussion

1. Why should the Christian practice temperance in all things?

_____

_____

2. What does temperance have to do with the Holy Spirit?

_____

_____

3. How does intemperance affect one's relationship with God?

_____

_____

4. List things in life that Christians can become intemperate in their practice.

_____

_____

5. List areas in your life in which you tend to be intemperate.

_____

_____

6. How do you plan to change the intemperate habits in your life?

_____

_____

Prayer Activity

● **Call your prayer partner and discuss this devotional with him/her.**
● **Pray with your prayer partner:**
  (1) for God to baptize you with His Holy Spirit.
  (2) for God to help you and your family to be temperate in all things so that you can better represent and serve God.
  (3) for the individuals on your prayer list.

Trust in Divine Power

Trust in divine power is the last natural remedy that Ellen White listed as a law of health: "Pure air, sunlight, abstemiousness, rest, exercise, proper diet, the use of water, *trust in divine power*—these are the true remedies" (*Counsels on Health,* p. 90; italics supplied).

Of all Christian denominations I am most familiar with the Seventh-day Adventist Church. I have been an Adventist for more than 45 years. As a people we pay attention to the first seven "true remedies" listed above. However, I find that the eighth one—trust in divine power—is often less known to us in its relationship to achieving good health. So let's consider how trust in divine power influences our physical well-being.

Throughout Christ's ministry we find that time and again He healed the sick. "God anointed Jesus of Nazareth with the Holy Ghost and with power: who went about doing good, and healing all that were oppressed of the devil; for God was with him" (Acts 10:38).

Matthew tells us why He did this: "When the even was come, they brought unto him many that were possessed with devils: and he cast out the spirits with his word, and healed all that were sick: That it might be fulfilled which was spoken by Esaias the prophet, saying, Himself took our infirmities, and bare our sicknesses" (Matt. 8:16, 17). Jesus paid the price for our physical healing on the cross, just as He did for our sins to be forgiven.

When He sent out His disciples, He enabled them to heal the sick.

"Then he called his twelve disciples together, and gave them power and authority over all devils, and to cure diseases. And he sent them to preach the kingdom of God, and to heal the sick" (Luke 9:1, 2).

We find that the church in the book of Acts followed Christ's example of healing the sick.

"And believers were the more added to the Lord, multitudes both of men and women (Acts 5:14). "Insomuch that they brought forth the sick into the streets, and laid them on beds and couches, that at the least the shadow of Peter passing by might overshadow some of them. There came also a multitude out of the cities round about unto Jerusalem, bringing sick folks, and them which were vexed with unclean spirits: and they were healed every one" (verses 15,16).

The apostle James instructed us: "Is any sick among you? let him call for the elders of the church; and let them pray over him, anointing him with oil in the name of the Lord: And the prayer of faith shall save the sick, and the Lord shall raise him up; and if he have committed sins, they shall be forgiven him" (James 5:14, 15).

Ellen White confirmed the importance of trust in divine power for restoration of one's physical health:

"If we are under infirmities of body, it is certainly consistent to trust in the Lord, making supplications to our God in our own case, and if we feel inclined to ask others in whom we have confidence to unite with us in prayer to Jesus who is the Mighty Healer, help will surely come if we ask in faith. I think we are altogether too faithless, too cold and lukewarm" (*Medical Ministry,* p. 16).

"When you neglect to offer prayer for the sick, you deprive them of great blessings; for angels of God are waiting to minister to these souls in response to your petitions" (*ibid.*, p. 195).

One does not have to be on their deathbed before having prayer for recovery from an illness. Also, we should do our best to follow God's health guidelines

65

when we seek Him for healing through prayer. For example, it would be presumptuous to pray for healing of cirrhosis of the liver and yet keep on drinking alcohol, or to pray for healing of lung cancer and continue to smoke. The prayer of faith for healing must include a life of faithfulness to God.

Personal Reflection and Discussion

1. What is the eighth of the eight true remedies Ellen White listed?

_____

_____

2. Why was Jesus able to heal the sick?

_____

_____

3. What did Jesus tell the disciples to do when He sent them out?

_____

_____

4. Why do you think Jesus connected healing the sick with preaching the gospel?

_____

_____

5. What did James say that we should do if we face sickness in our life?

_____

_____

6. What did Ellen White say about prayer for the sick?

_____

_____

7. What kind of lifestyle should the one being prayed for be seeking to follow?

_____

_____

Prayer Activity

- **Call your prayer partner and discuss this devotional with him/her.**
- **Pray with your prayer partner:**
    - **(1) for God to baptize you with His Holy Spirit.**
    - **(2) for God to give you faith to take your health problems to Him for healing.**
    - **(3) for the individuals on your prayer list.**

Fasting and Physical Health

Fasting is not only necessary in order to be stronger spiritually but it also enhances our physical health. Ellen White wrote: "There are some who would be benefited more by abstinence from food for a day or two every week than by any amount of treatment or medical advice. To fast one day a week would be of incalculable benefit to them" (*Counsels on Diet and Foods,* p. 189).

Good health plays an important role in our ability to hear God's voice better and overcome the enemy. Whatever negatively affects the body also has an adverse impact on the mind. It is through the mind that God communicates with us. Thus the clearer our mind, the better the communication is between us and God. This is why Satan attacks the minds of men, women, and youth today. I am convinced that is one primary reason he has inundated our society with mind-altering drugs as well as other substances and activities that distort the brain and its functioning.

Ellen White expanded the traditional definition of fasting. "The true fasting which should be recommended to all is abstinence from every stimulating kind of food, and the proper use of wholesome, simple food, which God has provided in abundance. Men need to think less of what they shall eat and drink of temporal food, and much more in regard to the food from heaven, that will give tone and vitality to the whole religious experience" (*Medical Ministry,* p. 283).

One major benefit of fasting is detoxification of our body. Detoxification is a process of the body eliminating or neutralizing poisonous substances through the colon, liver, kidneys, lungs, lymph glands, and skin. Fasting can trigger this, because when one fasts, it forces the body to use fat reserves for energy. The fat reserves store the toxins that we take into our bodies through various means. As the body burns its fat stores for energy, it releases the toxins and the body can then expel them.

Another benefit of fasting is that it promotes healing in the body. Energy not needed to digest food gets redirected to the metabolism and immune system. It can lead to the destruction of tumors and result in healthier cells, tissues, and organs. That is one reason animals stop eating when wounded, and humans lose hunger during certain illnesses such as influenza, gastritis, and tonsillitis.

A feeling of being energized often happens during times of fasting, plus life expectancy increases. For example, lab rats fed a very-low-calorie diet lived significantly longer than those on a higher-calorie diet. Researchers believe this happens because fasting produces a slower metabolic rate, improved immune system, more efficient protein production, and increased hormone production, including that of an antiaging hormone.

Fasting may improve rheumatoid arthritis, decrease allergic reactions such as hay fever and asthma, and help reduce edema in the lower body. In many cases it may lower high blood pressure. In addition, fasting makes it easier to overcome addictions such as tobacco and alcohol, and even aids the skin and eyes.

Good physical health plays an important role in one's relationship with God. Fasting brings both spiritual and physical benefits to those who choose to practice it. That is why those ready to meet Jesus will be a people who practice a regimen of fasting.

Personal Reflection and Discussion

1. What did Ellen White say about the physical benefits of fasting?

_____

_____

2. In what way did Ellen White expand the definition of fasting?

_____

_____

3. List some of the physical benefits of fasting.

_____

_____

4. How do the physical benefits of fasting help the Christian spiritually?

_____

_____

5. Why will those ready to meet Jesus be a people who practice fasting?

_____

_____

Prayer Activity

- Call your prayer partner and discuss this devotional with him/her.
- Pray with your prayer partner:
    (1) for God to baptize you with His Holy Spirit.
    (2) for God to help you and your family to be convicted of the benefits of fasting and to practice it as God leads.
    (3) for the individuals on your prayer list.

Day 30

Praising God and Health

An area that we may often overlook in relation to health is the importance of praising and rejoicing in the Lord. A thankful, joyful attitude toward God is highly conducive to well-being. God's Word clearly teaches this, and it applies to all that we are. Solomon wrote: "A merry heart doeth good like a medicine: but a broken spirit drieth the bones" (Prov. 17:22).

Medical science has observed that a thankful attitude plays an important role in achieving good health. *Pepperdine University Graziadio Business Review* (9, no. 4 [2006]) reported a positive relationship between thankfulness and a person's cardiovascular and immune system functions. "Grateful people take better care of themselves and engage in more protective health behaviors like regular exercise, a healthy diet, [and] regular physical examinations," according to University of California-Davis psychology professor Robert Emmons. Professor Emmons' research found that such individuals tend to be more optimistic, an attitude that boosts the immune system. Clinical psychologist Blair Justice, professor emeritus of psychology at the University of Texas School of Public Health at Houston, reports: "A growing body of research supports the notion that rediscovering a sense of abundance by thinking about those people and things we love lowers the risks of coronary events."

Ellen White wrote much on the importance of being thankful. "Courage, hope, faith, sympathy, love, promote health and prolong life. A contented mind, a cheerful spirit, is health to the body and strength to the soul" (*The Ministry of Healing*, p. 241).

In the Old Testament God made a highly significant statement concerning the relationship between joyful service to God and our prosperity and blessings from Him. He warned Israel that if they did not serve the Lord with "joyfulness, and with gladness of heart, for the abundance of all things" that He had given them, they would be defeated by their enemies (Deut. 28:47, 48). Thus a negative, sorrowful, unthankful attitude in life is actually a sin against God. If we desire spiritual, emotional, and physical blessings and prosperity from God, we must by His grace maintain a joyful, thankful, praising attitude toward Him.

David understood this when he wrote: "I will bless the Lord at all times: his praise shall continually be in my mouth" (Ps. 34:1). Daniel faced a most difficult situation when the Persian Empire issued a law that no one was to pray to anyone except King Darius. Yet the prophet continued his practice of praying three times a day in plain sight with his window open. Scripture records that Daniel "prayed, and gave thanks before his God" (Dan. 6:10). He knew the importance of an attitude of continual praise and thanksgiving toward God even when facing such a serious threat.

We find the same kind of examples in the New Testament. The apostle Paul faced many challenges in his life and service for the Lord. He tells us that he received 39 stripes from the Jews five times and was imprisoned, beaten with rods three times, stoned once, shipwrecked three times, threatened by robbers, often hungry and thirsty, at times cold and naked, and betrayed by false believers (2 Cor. 11:23-27). If any servant of the Lord had reason to complain and become unthankful, he seems to top the list. Yet he has some of the most positive counsel about the importance of a thankful, joyful attitude toward the Lord.

"For I have learned, in whatsoever state I am, therewith to be content. I know both how to be abased, and I know how to abound: every where and in all things I am instructed both to be full and to be hungry, both to abound and to suffer need" (Phil. 4:11, 12).

Why was he able to have such a confident, positive attitude under such difficult circumstances? "I can do all things through Christ which strengtheneth me" (verse 13). When he and Silas were put in prison with their feet in stocks, we read that "Paul and Silas prayed, and sang praises unto God" (Acts 16:25).

It was Paul who counseled Christians to "rejoice in the Lord always: and again I say, Rejoice" (Phil. 4:4), and to "rejoice evermore. . . . In every thing give thinks: for this is the will of God in Christ Jesus concerning you" (1 Thess. 5:16-18).

Why did he have such a meaningful relationship with Christ? How could he sing praises to God while in chains in prison? At the very beginning of his call to serve the Lord he received the baptism of the Holy Spirit (Acts 9:17). He continued to experience the Spirit's infilling every day (Eph. 5:18). And remember, love, joy, and peace are the first fruit of the Spirit listed (Gal. 5:22, 23).

Personal Reflection and Discussion

1. What does the Old Testament say about the importance of maintaining a thankful, praising attitude toward God?

_____

_____

2. What are some physical benefits of a praising and thankful attitude?

_____

_____

3. What severe warning did God give Israel if they did not serve Him with joyfulness and gladness?

_____

_____

4. What New Testament examples do we have of God's children praising Him even in difficult times?

_____

_____

5. How was Paul able to have an attitude of praise and thanksgiving while in prison?

_____

_____

Prayer Activity

● **Call your prayer partner and discuss this devotional with him/her.**
● **Pray with your prayer partner:**
  (1) for God to baptize you with His Holy Spirit.
  (2) for God to help you and your family to maintain an attitude of praise and thanksgiving toward God in all situations.
  (3) for the individuals on your prayer list.

Anger and Health

The Bible has some significant counsels on anger. "He that is slow to anger is better than the mighty; and he that ruleth his spirit than he that taketh a city" (Prov. 16:32). "Follow peace with all men, and holiness, without which no man shall see the Lord: Looking diligently lest any man fail of the grace of God; lest any root of bitterness springing up trouble you, and thereby many be defiled" (Heb. 12:14, 15).

Ellen White also wrote about the dangers of anger.

"How Satan exults when he is enabled to set the soul into a white heat of anger! A glance, a gesture, an intonation, may be seized upon and used, as the arrow of Satan, to wound and poison the heart that is open to receive it.

"When one once gives place to an angry spirit he is just as much intoxicated as the man who has put the glass to his lips.

"Christ treats anger as murder. . . . Passionate words are a savor of death unto death. He who utters them is not cooperating with God to save his fellow man. In heaven this wicked railing is placed in the same list as common swearing. While hatred is cherished in the soul there is not one iota of the love of God there" (*Our High Calling,* p. 235).

There is no sin in feeling anger. The issue is what one does with those feelings. The apostle Paul advised: "Be ye angry, and sin not: let not the sun go down upon your wrath: Neither give place to the devil" (Eph. 4:26, 27). Here we discover that anger actually gives Satan a foothold in our lives.

Holding on to anger has negative physiological affects. Prolonged anger will chronically stimulate the body's survival systems, which includes the androgenic hormone system as well as the immune system. It is the adrenal gland that produces such anger associated hormones. Research shows that constant stimulation of the adrenal system will result in higher blood pressure and cholesterol levels.

The body's adrenal system has to rest for a while after being stimulated by anger. If this does not happen because of continuing rage, the body will begin to break down. It can lead to heart disease and the immune system temporarily shutting down. Therefore, angry people are more likely to get sick. For example, studies show that those with unhappy marriages catch more colds. Evidence even indicates that chronic anger increases the chances of cancer developing in the body.

Risk factors for heart disease are directly related to the fight-or-flight response caused by anger. Heart disease, high blood pressure, lipid metabolism changes, diabetes, pulmonary problems, slower healing of wounds, and heart attacks all have a clear emotional link.

Unresolved anger also causes many emotional problems such as depression, sadness, fear, etc. All such emotions add to physical health problems as well as have a negative impact on one's spiritual relationship with God.

The solution is to daily be filled with God's Spirit through which Christ lives in us. We must learn how to let Him manifest His love, joy, and peace in our hearts. God's love filling our hearts will cast out all fear, anger, and depression, and we will have joy and peace. Above all, we need to have the experience that Paul described:

"I am crucified with Christ: nevertheless I live; yet not I, but Christ liveth in me: and the life which I now live in the flesh I live by the faith of the Son of God, who loved me, and gave himself for me" (Gal. 2:20).

Personal Reflection and Discussion

1. What is the Bible's instruction about clinging to anger?

_____

_____

2. What did Ellen White say about the dangers of anger?

_____

_____

3. What are some of the physical health problems associated with harboring anger?

_____

_____

4. What are some of the negative emotions associated with keeping anger?

_____

_____

5. What is the solution to getting rid of anger?

_____

_____

Prayer Activity

- **Call your prayer partner and discuss this devotional with him/her.**
- **Pray with your prayer partner:**
    - **(1) for God to baptize you with His Holy Spirit.**
    - **(2) for God to help you and your family to let go of anger and let Christ manifest His love, joy, and peace in your hearts.**
    - **(3) for the individuals on your prayer list.**

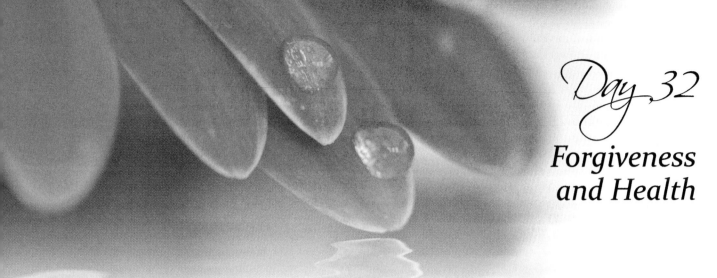

The Bible is extremely clear about the necessity for a Christian to forgive those who have wronged them. "And when ye stand praying, forgive, if ye have ought against any: that your Father also which is in heaven may forgive you your trespasses. But if ye do not forgive, neither will your Father which is in heaven forgive your trespasses" (Mark 11:25, 26).

God commands us to forgive because refusing to do so hinders our relationship with Him and will cause us physical and emotional health problems. To hang on to an unforgiving attitude is to place our eternal destiny in jeopardy.

"Follow peace with all men, and holiness, without which no man shall see the Lord: Looking diligently lest any man fail of the grace of God; lest any root of bitterness springing up trouble you, and thereby many be defiled" (Heb. 12:14, 15).

God's Word is clear. Choosing not to forgive someone will lead to our eternal destruction and may even influence others to reject God.

An article in an issue of *Harvard Women's Health Watch* stated: "Not only is being able to forgive divine, it can be a blessing to your mental and physical health" (January 2005). An unforgiving attitude produces the same body reactions as a major stressful event. It leads to tense muscles, higher blood pressure, and increased perspiration. Forgiveness, on the other hand, reduces stress and improves the heart rate and blood pressure. It can even lessen some body pains.

A study published in the *Personality and Social Psychology Bulletin* found that forgiveness restores a negative relationship to a positive one with the individual forgiven. Plus forgiveness will affect one's attitude toward others, which will enhance other social relationships. For example, forgiveness even makes one more willing to volunteer and donate to good causes.

As Christians we have no right to hang on to anger toward anyone no matter what they have done to us. Just as God has forgiven us, so we are to forgive others. The issue is really one of pride. Often we become unforgiving and angry because of wounded pride.

"It is the love of self that destroys our peace. While self is all alive, we stand ready continually to guard it from mortification and insult; but when we are dead, and our life is hid with Christ in God, we shall not take neglects or slights to heart. We shall be deaf to reproach and blind to scorn and insult" (*Thoughts From the Mount of Blessing,* p. 16).

"When we possess true meekness and lowliness we are so lost in Christ that we do not take neglect or slights to heart; we are deaf to reproach and blind to scorn and insult" (*Testimonies for the Church,* vol. 2, p. 567).

The real issue is love. We are naturally unloving and unforgiving. However, when we are filled with God's Spirit His love will be "shed abroad in our hearts by the Holy Ghost" (Rom. 5:5). Such love will manifest itself in the following way toward others.

"Love is very patient and kind, never jealous or envious, never boastful or proud, never haughty or selfish or rude. Love does not demand its own way. It is not irritable or touchy. It does not hold grudges and will hardly even notice when others do it wrong. It is never glad about injustice, but rejoices whenever truth wins out. If you love someone you will be loyal to him no matter what the cost. You will always believe in him, always expect the best of him, and always stand your ground in defending him" (1 Cor. 13:4-7, TLB).

Therefore, when tempted to be unforgiving, we must ask Christ to manifest His love, compassion, and forgiveness in us toward the one who has wronged us. In this manner we will be allowing Christ to reveal His character of love in and through us, which will be the experience of all who are ready to meet Jesus when He returns. As a result, forgiveness has both temporal and eternal benefits to ourselves and to others.

Personal Reflection and Discussion

1. What is the Bible's instruction concerning an unforgiving attitude?

_____

_____

2. What are some of the physical health problems associated with harboring unforgiveness?

_____

_____

3. What are some of the negative emotions associated with unforgiveness?

_____

_____

4. What did Ellen White say about unforgiveness?

_____

_____

5. What are the eternal consequences of maintaining an unforgiving attitude?

_____

_____

6. What is the solution to getting rid of an unforgiving attitude?

_____

_____

Prayer Activity

- **Call your prayer partner and discuss this devotional with him/her.**
- **Pray with your prayer partner:**
    - **(1) for God to baptize you with His Holy Spirit.**
    - **(2) for God to help you and your family to forgive those who have hurt you.**
    - **(3) for God to help you learn how to let Christ manifest His love, compassion, and forgiveness in and through you.**
    - **(4) for the individuals on your prayer list.**

Stress and Health

In Genesis we read that God created human beings to live in the Garden of Eden.

"And the Lord God planted a garden eastward in Eden; and there he put the man whom he had formed" (Gen. 2:8).

Thus the Lord did not intend humanity to carry a heavy load of stress. Instead He designed them to dwell in a pleasant environment in which their relationships would be positive and work pleasurable. The Garden of Eden was a worry-free environment.

That, of course, is not the situation in which we find ourselves today. We live in a world filled with stress and anxiety. Economic downturns, job loss, and family conflict all create stress in our lives. Since God did not create us to carry such negative life burdens, they will lead to health problems. Stress triggers the fight-or-flight mechanism in the body. As a result it releases adrenalin and cortisol, hormones that speed up the heart rate, slow digestion, and direct blood to certain muscle groups that prepare the body to deal with a crisis or threat. The stressor will also change the autonomic nervous functions.

Chronic stressful situations such as a bad marriage or a negative work environment will trigger the body to continue to produce adrenaline and cortisol. The constant presence of the hormones will lead to a variety of health problems, such as depression, diabetes, heart disease, hyperthyroidism, obesity, obsessive-compulsive and anxiety disorders, sexual dysfunction, and ulcers, and the potential for cancer by reducing the white blood cells that fight cancer cells. Because constant stress suppresses the immune system, the individual becomes more susceptible to disease. It also leads to an imbalance between oxidants and antioxidants in the body, which will accelerate the aging process.

Health professionals estimate that stress causes 90 percent of the physical problems that patients see their doctor for. Ellen White confirmed this when she wrote: "The relation that exists between the mind and the body is very intimate. When one is affected, the other sympathizes. The condition of the mind affects the health to a far greater degree than many realize. Many of the diseases from which men suffer are the result of mental depression. Grief, anxiety, discontent, remorse, guilt, distrust, all tend to break down the life forces and to invite decay and death" (*The Ministry of Healing,* p. 241).

Repeated stress can also lead to the use of tobacco, alcohol, and other drugs as ways to deal with it. Also, eating disorders can develop as a result. All of the effects of chronic stress will hinder our relationship with God.

But our Creator has provided a solution. Again and again the Bible instructs us to look to Him, trust in Him, and depend on Him to provide for our every need. Jesus clearly taught this important truth when He pointed out that our heavenly Father even provides for the birds of the air and the flowers of the field. He then concludes with the instruction: "Therefore take no thought, saying, What shall we eat? or, What shall we drink? or, Wherewithal shall we be clothed? (For after all these things do the Gentiles seek:) for your heavenly Father knoweth that ye have need of all these things. But seek ye first the kingdom of God, and his righteousness; and all these things shall be added unto you. Take therefore no thought for the morrow: for the morrow shall take thought for the things of itself. Sufficient unto the day is the evil thereof" (Matt. 6:31-34).

Instead of worrying about life's cares, we are to let our heavenly Father provide for us. We are not to worry about our future. It is in God's hands, and He promises to work everything out for us. "And we know that all things work together for good to them that love God, to them who are the called according to his purpose" (Rom. 8:28).

So instead of worrying about the things in life that heap stress upon us, we need to take them to God in prayer and trust that He will work everything out in ways that are best for us, and then keep focusing on our blessings and God's promises.

"Be careful for nothing; but in every thing by prayer and supplication with thanksgiving let your requests be made known unto God. And the peace of God, which passeth all understanding, shall keep your hearts and minds through Christ Jesus. Finally, brethren, whatsoever things are true, whatsoever things are honest, whatsoever things are just, whatsoever things are pure, whatsoever things are lovely, whatsoever things are of good report; if there be any virtue, and if there be any praise, think on these things" (Phil. 4:6-8).

Personal Reflection and Discussion

1. **What kind of environment did God create human beings to live in?**

_____

_____

2. **What kind of environment do we actually have today?**

_____

_____

3. **What physical conditions can develop if we live with chronic stress?**

_____

_____

4. **What emotional problems can surface if we live with chronic stress?**

_____

_____

5. **How will chronic stress affect our faith in God?**

_____

6. **What solution has God given us to deal with chronic stress?**

_____

Prayer Activity

- **Call your prayer partner and discuss this devotional with him/her.**
- **Pray with your prayer partner:**
    (1) for God to baptize you with His Holy Spirit.
    (2) for God to help you and your family to learn to trust Him instead of focusing on the things that cause stress in your life.
    (3) for the individuals on your prayer list.

Day 34

Fear and Health

God's Word instructs us not to give in to fear. "Fear thou not; for I am with thee: be not dismayed; for I am thy God: I will strengthen thee; yea, I will help thee; yea, I will uphold thee with the right hand of my righteousness. . . . For I the Lord thy God will hold thy right hand, saying unto thee, Fear not; I will help thee" (Isa. 41:10-13).

When Jesus and the disciples were in the boat during the storm on the Sea of Galilee, He asked them an amazing question considering the circumstances they were in: "Why are ye fearful, O ye of little faith?" (Matt. 8:26).

Ellen White commented on Christ's reaction to the life-threatening storm. "When Jesus was awakened to meet the storm, He was in perfect peace. There was no trace of fear in word or look, for no fear was in His heart. But He rested not in the possession of almighty power. It was not as the 'Master of earth and sea and sky' that He reposed in quiet. That power He had laid down, and He says, 'I can of Mine own self do nothing.' John 5:30. He trusted in the Father's might. It was in faith—faith in God's love and care—that Jesus rested, and the power of that word which stilled the storm was the power of God" (*The Desire of Ages,* p. 336).

Fear is deadly to our physical, emotional, and spiritual well-being. Don Colbert, M.D., wrote: "Fear has been associated with a wide variety of diseases, including cardiovascular diseases and hypertension; digestive-tract diseases such as colitis, Crohn's disease, irritable bowel syndrome, and ulcers; headaches; and skin disorders such as psoriasis, eczema, and stress acne. Fear can cause a decreased immune response, which may lead to frequent infections or development of deadly diseases. Fear can produce a heart attack . . . or even death" (*Deadly Emotions,* p. 95).

During the last days fear will be a common emotion. Jesus warned of "men's hearts failing them for fear" (Luke 21:26). The book of Revelation points out that it will be a characteristic of those who are not ready when Jesus returns.

"He that overcometh shall inherit all things; and I will be his God, and he shall be my son. But *the fearful,* and unbelieving, and the abominable, and murderers, and whoremongers, and sorcerers, and idolaters, and all liars, shall have their part in the lake which burneth with fire and brimstone: which is the second death." (Rev. 21:7, 8).

On the other hand, those ready to meet Jesus will have the "love of God shed . . . abroad in [their] hearts by the Holy Ghost" (Rom. 5:5), something that happens as we daily receive the baptism of the Holy Spirit. Because of this all fear will vanish. Why? Because "there is no fear in love; but perfect love casteth out fear: because fear hath torment. He that feareth is not made perfect in love" (1 John 4:18).

Commenting further on the storm experience of the disciples and their lack of faith, Ellen White observed:

"As Jesus rested by faith in the Father's care, so we are to rest in the care of our Savior. If the disciples had trusted in Him, they would have been kept in peace. Their fear in the time of danger revealed their unbelief. In their efforts to save themselves, they forgot Jesus; and it was only when, in despair of self-dependence, they turned to Him that He could give them help.

"How often the disciples' experience is ours! When the tempests of temptation gather, and the fierce lightnings flash, and the waves sweep over us, we battle with the storm alone, forgetting that there is One who can help us. We trust in our own strength till our hope is lost, and we are ready to perish. Then we remember Jesus, and if we call upon Him to save us, we shall not cry in vain. . . .Whether on the land or on the sea, if we have the Savior in our hearts, there is no need of fear. Living faith in the Redeemer will smooth the sea of life, and will deliver us from danger in the way that He knows to be best" (*The Desire of Ages,* p. 336).

Personal Reflection and Discussion

1. What are some of the negative consequences of fear?

_____

_____

2. What does fear reveal about our relationship with God?

_____

_____

3. What are the characteristics of those not ready to meet Jesus?

_____

_____

4. Why will it be essential that those ready to meet Jesus have no fear?

_____

_____

5. What do we need in order not to fear?

_____

_____

Prayer Activity

- **Call your prayer partner and discuss this devotional with him/her.**
- **Pray with your prayer partner:**
    (1) for God to baptize you with His Holy Spirit.
    (2) for God to help you and your family to learn to trust Him instead of becoming fearful in difficult situations.
    (3) for the individuals on your prayer list.

Day 35

Fasting and Defeating Satan

We read about an encounter between good and evil forces that took place when a father brought his son to Jesus' disciples and asked them to deliver the son from an evil spirit that possessed him. The disciples had, in the name of Jesus, cast out demons before: "And when he had called unto him his twelve disciples, he gave them power against unclean spirits, to cast them out, and to heal all manner of sickness and all manner of disease" (Matt. 10:1). However, this time they were unable to rid the boy of the evil spirit. "And when they were come to the multitude, there came to him a certain man, kneeling down to him, and saying, Lord, have mercy on my son: for he is a lunatic, and sore vexed: for ofttimes he falleth into the fire, and oft into the water. And I brought him to thy disciples, and they could not cure him" (Matt. 17:14-16). The father then brought his son to Jesus. Responding to the father's plea, Jesus "rebuked the devil; and he departed out of him: and the child was cured" (verse 18).

Confused and puzzled, the disciples asked Jesus why they were unable to expel the demon. Jesus said: "Because of your unbelief. . . . Howbeit this kind goeth not out but by prayer and fasting" (verses 20, 21).

Since Jesus indicated that the evil spirit was more powerful and resistant, it appears that the disciples had not encountered a similar one before. They had had no problem dealing with spirits in previous encounters. This one, however, required something more in order to be driven out. Jesus stated that the situation demanded "fasting and prayer."

Is fasting a mandatory requirement in order to cast out some evil spirits and advance God's kingdom? Let's let the Bible answer.

When Jesus faced the demon in the child, He did not at that moment pray and fast. However, we know that at the beginning of His ministry He did experience an intense time of prayer and fasting. "Then was Jesus led up of the Spirit into the wilderness to be tempted of the devil. And when he had fasted forty days and forty nights, he was afterward an hungered" (Matt. 4:1, 2). This time of fasting and prayer had a specific purpose. Jesus knew that both were mandatory in order for Him to defeat Satan.

Christ's prayer and fasting prepared Him for the wilderness temptations and the ministry that lay ahead of Him. They were necessary in order to gain the greatest victories over temptation and sin.

"When Christ was the most fiercely beset by temptation, He ate nothing [fasted]. He committed Himself to God, and through earnest prayer, and perfect submission to the will of His Father, came off conqueror. Those who profess the truth for these last days, above every other class of professed Christians, should imitate the great Exemplar in prayer" (*Counsels on Diet and Foods,* p. 186).

What does she say we must do? That we must imitate Christ. What specific part of Christ's life does she point out as our example? That in order to live a victorious life as Christ did and defeat Satan each time we encounter him, we must follow Christ's example of fasting and prayer. This is exactly what the Bible teaches us also. "For even hereunto were ye called: because Christ also suffered for us, leaving us an example, that ye should follow his steps" (1 Peter 2:21).

After the disciples had fasted and prayed for 10 days the Spirit filled them on the day of Pentecost. The power of God was so strong with the disciples that the gospel spread throughout the known world, and in the process they healed the sick, drove out demons, and raised the dead.

Ellen White advised the church that "we cannot have a weak faith now; we cannot be safe in a listless, indolent, slothful attitude. Every jot of ability is to be used, and sharp, calm, deep thinking is to be done. The wisdom of any human agent is not sufficient for the planning and devising in this time. Spread every plan before God with fasting, [and] with the humbling of the soul before the Lord Jesus, and commit thy ways unto the Lord" (*Selected Messages,* book 2, p. 364). Those ready to meet Jesus will be a people of fasting and prayer.

Personal Reflection and Discussion

1. **What happened when the disciples tried to cast out the demon in the child that the father had brought to them?**

   _____

   _____

2. **What did Jesus say was the reason they could not drive out the evil spirit?**

   _____

   _____

3. **Did Jesus have a life that included fasting and prayer?**

   _____

   _____

4. **What does this story teach us about those who will be ready to meet Jesus?**

   _____

   _____

Prayer Activity

- **Call your prayer partner and discuss this devotional with him/her.**
- **Pray with your prayer partner:**
    - **(1) for God to baptize you with His Holy Spirit.**
    - **(2) for God to help you and your family enter into a spiritual life that includes fasting and prayer.**
    - **(3) for the individuals on your prayer list.**

The Temple Restored

The prophet Ezekiel foretold the restoration of God's temple and that a river of healing would flow from it. The river begins very small and grows into a great torrent. Everywhere it goes it brings healing and life.

"Afterward he brought me again unto the door of the house [temple]; and, behold, waters issued out from under the threshold of the house eastward: for the forefront of the house stood toward the east, and the waters came down from under from the right side of the house, at the south side of the altar. . . . And when the man that had the line in his hand went forth eastward, he measured a thousand cubits, and he brought me through the waters; the waters were to the ankles. Again he measured a thousand, and brought me through the waters; the waters were to the knees. Again he measured a thousand, and brought me through; the waters were to the loins. Afterward he measured a thousand; and it was a river that I could not pass over: for the waters were risen, waters to swim in, a river that could not be passed over. And he said unto me, Son of man, hast thou seen this? Then he brought me, and caused me to return to the brink of the river. . . . Then said he unto me, These waters issue out toward the east country, and go down into the desert, and go into the sea: which being brought forth into the sea, the waters shall be healed. And it shall come to pass, that every thing that liveth, which moveth, whithersoever the rivers shall come, shall live: and there shall be a very great multitude of fish, because these waters shall come thither: for they shall be healed; and every thing shall live whither the river cometh" (Eze. 47:1-9).

In the New Testament the temple is the church and God's people. "Know ye not that ye are the temple of God, and that the Spirit of God dwelleth in you?" (1 Cor. 3:16). Therefore, when we correctly apply the temple prophecy of Ezekiel to the New Testament church, we realize that a great work of healing and deliverance will proceed within and from the church into the world just before Jesus returns.

Jesus stated this very truth and applied it to Christians: "He that believeth on me, as the scripture hath said, out of his belly shall flow rivers of living water" (John 7:38). John then clarifies that those who receive the baptism of the Holy Spirit will conduct such a ministry. "But this spake he of the Spirit, which they that believe on him should receive: for the Holy Ghost was not yet given, because that Jesus was not yet glorified" (verse 39).

The Old Testament Temple represented God's character in every detail of its construction and services. God's glorious presence filled the earthly structure. God's New Testament temple—His people and church—are to be and do the same, being filled with His presence and representing His character. It happens as God's people experience the baptism of the Holy Spirit and righteousness by faith in Christ alone. Furthermore, they let God "cleanse" His earthly temple, which is His people and church, by bringing physical, emotional, and spiritual healing. That is why following practices that achieve good health are so important in the last days. We are to become vessels in whom God can dwell and communicate to and through to others. For it to take place to the fullest extent requires good physical, emotional, and spiritual health. God's last-day people will understand and practice the principles of good health because they know it is the only way to be in such close relationship with Him that they will victoriously make it through the final crisis and be ready for Christ's return.

Ellen White wrote, "Wonderful is the work which the Lord designs to accomplish through His church, that His name may be glorified. A picture of this work is given in Ezekiel's vision of the river of healing [she then quotes Ezekiel 47:8-12]" (*The Acts of the Apostles,* p. 13). Elsewhere, after quoting Zechariah 13:1, she declares, "The waters of this fountain contain medicinal properties that will heal both physical and spiritual infirmities. From this fountain flows the mighty river seen in Ezekiel's vision [she then quotes Ezekiel 47:8-12]" (*Testimonies for the Church,* vol. 6, pp. 227, 228).

Personal Reflection and Discussion

1. What is the temple of God in the New Testament?

_____

2. What did the prophet Ezekiel say would take place in and through the temple of God in the last days?

_____

3. What did Jesus say was necessary for His people to experience in order to have rivers of living water flowing from them?

_____

_____

4. Whose character did the Old Testament Temple portray?

_____

5. Whose character must the New Testament temple, or church, reveal?

_____

6. What role does following health principles play in God's being able to reveal His character in and through His people?

_____

Prayer Activity

- **Call your prayer partner and discuss this devotional with him/her.**
- **Pray with your prayer partner:**
    (1) for God to baptize you with His Holy Spirit.
    (2) for God to help you and your family understand and practice the laws of health so that God can reveal His character in and through you.
    (3) for the individuals on your prayer list.

Day 37

The Right Arm of Preparation

The focus of this devotional book has been on the role that the laws of health will play in preparing God's people for Christ's second coming. Not only are they to help get the church ready for the Second Advent, but also God will use them to lead others in that same preparation. Paul clearly pointed out that what we eat and drink will affect how fully God will be able to manifest His character in and through us. "Whether therefore ye eat, or drink, or whatsoever ye do, do all to the glory of God" (1 Cor. 10:31).

Christ came to reveal the Father's glory: "And the Word was made flesh, and dwelt among us, (and we beheld his glory, the glory as of the only begotten of the Father,) full of grace and truth" (John 1:14). He did it in two ways. First, He reflected the character of the Father in His life. That is why he told Philip that "he that hath seen me hath seen the Father" (John 14:9).

The second way Christ depicted the Father's character was through ministering to others in love. "And Jesus went about all Galilee, teaching in their synagogues, and preaching the gospel of the kingdom, and healing all manner of sickness and all manner of disease among the people" (Matt. 4:23). In fact, when we study the life of Christ we find that He healed more than He taught and preached. Therefore, healing plays an important role in portraying the divine character.

Jesus said that His followers would do the same work of bringing healing to others as He did. "Verily, verily, I say unto you, He that believeth on me, the works that I do shall he do also; and greater works than these shall he do; because I go unto my Father" (John 14:12). Notice that Jesus said it would happen because He would go to the Father. As a result, the baptism of the Holy Spirit became available to every believer. It is through the Spirit's in-filling that Jesus lives in them. Jesus referred to this same truth when He said, "He that believeth on me, as the scripture hath said, out of his belly shall flow rivers of living water" (John 7:38). Here Jesus foretold that a message and ministry of health would issue from His people. John interpreted Jesus' words in the next verse: "But this spake he of the Spirit, which they that believe on him should receive: for the Holy Ghost was not yet given; because that Jesus was not yet glorified" (verse 39).

The meaning is that Jesus will live in believers through the baptism of the Holy Spirit and will seek to manifest a ministry of healing through them. This is vital during the last days, because physical, emotional, and spiritual health are essential for God's people to be ready for Christ's return. A message of health and healing will be part of the gospel. That is exactly what Jesus did—He taught, preached, and healed.

In order for us to participate in a last-day health ministry, we ourselves must understand and practice its principles. God will then be better able to use us to minister to others. Ellen White understood this when she wrote:

"Again and again I have been instructed that the medical missionary work is to bear the same relation to the work of the third angel's message that the arm and hand bear to the body. Under the direction of the divine Head they are to work unitedly in preparing the way for the coming of Christ. The right arm of the body of truth is to be constantly active, constantly at work, and God will strengthen it" (*Testimonies for the Church,* vol. 6, p. 288).

The principles of health are to prepare God's people for Christ's second coming as well as to reach out to others. Therefore, we must understand and practice health ourselves in order to be a part of God's closing work on earth.

Personal Reflection and Discussion

1. What are the two purposes of the health message?

_____

_____

2. How did Christ reveal the Father's glory, or character?

_____

_____

3. What did Jesus say that those who believed in Him would do?

_____

_____

4. Why is it essential that the believer experience the daily baptism of the Holy Spirit in order to do the ministry of healing that Christ said would take place?

_____

_____

5. What did Ellen White call the medical missionary program?

_____

_____

Prayer Activity

- Call your prayer partner and discuss this devotional with him/her.
- Pray with your prayer partner:
    (1) for God to baptize you with His Holy Spirit.
    (2) for God to help you and your family understand and practice the laws of physical, emotional, and spiritual health so that God can use you more effectively to ready others for Christ's soon return.
    (3) for the individuals on your prayer list.

The Purpose of Good Health

For the Christian, obeying the laws of physical, emotional, and spiritual health goes much deeper than simply seeking to achieve health for its own sake. Many non-Christians also follow health principles, but for other reasons. For example, many involved in spiritualism, witchcraft, New Age teachings, etc., practice health principles and even fasting in order to "become attuned with the higher self, thus facilitating the higher self's emergence into the physical realm and bringing the practitioner under the guidance and direction of [God]" (Ray Yungen, *A Time of Departing,* p. 23).

Instead, the Christian seeks physical, emotional, and spiritual health to be in the best possible condition for God to reveal His glory (character) in and through them: "Whether therefore ye eat, or drink, or whatsoever ye do, do all to the glory of God" (1 Cor. 10:31).

Just before Jesus returns, God will display His glory on earth. "And after these things I saw another angel come down from heaven, having great power; and the earth was lightened with his glory" (Rev. 18:1).

Through the experience of the daily baptism of the Holy Spirit, Christ lives in the one who seeks the Spirit's infilling. Our Savior will lead us to the point at which He is being manifest in us more and more every day.

"But we all, with open face beholding as in a glass the glory of the Lord, are changed into the same image from glory to glory, even as by the Spirit of the Lord" (2 Cor. 3:18).

Here is the real goal for good physical, emotional, and spiritual health. We are to cooperate with God in removing the obstacles in our life that hinder this from happening to the fullest extent. If we ignore the laws of our physical well-being, our minds will be unable to receive from God all that He wants to communicate to us. Negative emotional issues will hinder Christ from revealing Himself in us as He desires. And ignoring the principles that enable us to be strong spiritually will greatly weaken our relationship with Christ. As a result we will be choosing not to enter into the experience that Paul described as: "I am crucified with Christ: nevertheless I live; yet not I, but Christ liveth in me: and the life which I now live in the flesh I live by the faith of the Son of God, who loved me, and gave himself for me" (Gal. 2:20).

Also, if we ignore these principles, we will not be the vessels that Jesus can use to reveal Himself to the world or the instruments that He employs to bring the same healing we are to experience to others in preparation for Christ's second coming. Jesus symbolically spoke of this when He said: "He that believeth on me, as the scripture hath said, out of his belly shall flow rivers of living water" (John 7:38).

Those ready to meet Jesus will reflect His character. "Beloved, now are we the sons of God, and it doth not yet appear what we shall be: but we know that, when he shall appear, we shall be like him; for we shall see him as he is" (1 John 3:2). The reason for this is that it is Jesus manifested in them. It is what Christ seeks to take place in His followers. The total health message will play an important role in the process of transformation.

"Christ is waiting with longing desire for the manifestation of Himself in His church. When the character of Christ shall be perfectly reproduced in His people, then He will come to claim them as His own" (*Christ's Object Lessons,* p. 69).

Personal Reflection and Discussion

1. Why do many non-Christians follow health principles?

_____

_____

2. Why should Christians take seriously God's laws of health?

_____

_____

3. How will poor physical health affect our relationship with God?

_____

_____

4. How will poor emotional health affect our relationship with God?

_____

_____

5. What is Christ waiting for before He returns?

_____

_____

Prayer Activity

- Call your prayer partner and discuss this devotional with him/her.
- Pray with your prayer partner:
    (1) for God to baptize you with His Holy Spirit.
    (2) for God to help you and your family understand and practice the laws of physical, emotional, and spiritual health so that Christ can manifest Himself fully in your lives.
    (3) for the individuals on your prayer list.

A Purification Time

The prophet Daniel wrote that at the very end of time "shall Michael stand up, the great prince which standeth for the children of thy people: and there shall be a time of trouble, such as never was since there was a nation even to that same time: and at that time thy people shall be delivered, every one that shall be found written in the book" (Dan. 12:1). The judgment will end, symbolized by Michael's standing up. Then the tribulation or time of trouble will immediately follow. When the conflict between Christ and Satan and between Christ's followers and the antichrist reaches its peak, God intervenes to deliver His people—"every one that shall be found written in the book [of life]."

When the judgment ceases every case will have been decided as to who is saved and who is lost. "He that is unjust, let him be unjust still: and he which is filthy, let him be filthy still: and he that is righteous, let him be righteous still: and he that is holy, let him be holy still. And, behold, I come quickly; and my reward is with me, to give every man according as his work shall be" (Rev. 22:11, 12). It must all take place before Jesus returns since there is no second chance for salvation after the Second Advent.

Since the judgment has ceased, God's people will be living without Christ as their mediator. John the revelator also portrayed this when he pointed to a time when the temple (sanctuary) in heaven was closed. "And the temple was filled with smoke from the glory of God, and from his power; and no man was able to enter into the temple, till the seven plagues of the seven angels were fulfilled" (Rev. 15:8).

By then Christ must be manifested 100 percent in each of our lives. We must fully experience righteous-ness by faith. As God's people we must come to where we have learned how to let Jesus live out His life of victory completely in our lives. We must come to where we do not sin in thought, word, or deed. Ellen White described this condition. " 'The prince of this world cometh,' said Jesus, 'and hath nothing in me.' John 14:30. There was in Him nothing that responded to Satan's sophistry. He did not consent to sin. Not even by a thought did He yield to temptation. So it may be with us" (*The Desire of Ages,* p. 123).

If we want to be ready for that time, all of us must prepare for it by understanding and experiencing the daily baptism of the Holy Spirit and righteousness by faith in Christ alone and following daily God's counsels on attaining physical, emotional, and spiritual health. Each day we must enter into those experiences that will enable God to do the purifying work described in Malachi 3:1-4 in preparation for Christ's return. Christ will then be fully living out His life in the lives of His people. This is why John could write, "Beloved, now are we the sons of God, and it doth not yet appear what we shall be: but we know that, when he shall appear, we shall be like him; for we shall see him as he is" (1 John 3:2). God's people at that time are just like Jesus, because it is Jesus manifest in and through them.

Ellen White described this purification time. "Says the prophet: 'Who may abide the day of his coming? and who shall stand when he appeareth? for he is like a refiner's fire, and like fullers' soap: and he shall sit as a refiner and purifier of silver: and he shall purify the sons of Levi, and purge them as gold and silver, that they may offer unto the Lord an offering in righteous-ness.' Malachi 3:2, 3. Those who are living upon the earth when the intercession of Christ shall cease in the sanctuary above are to stand in the sight of a holy God without a mediator. Their robes must be spotless, their characters must be purified from sin by the blood of sprinkling. Through the grace of God and their own diligent effort they must be conquerors in the battle with evil. While the investigative judgment is going forward in heaven, while the sins of penitent believers are being removed from the sanctuary, there is to be a special work of purification, of putting away of sin, among God's people upon earth. This work is more clearly presented in the messages of Revelation 14.

"When this work shall have been accomplished, the followers of Christ will be ready for his appearing. 'Then shall the offering of Judah and Jerusalem be pleasant unto the Lord, as in the days of old, and as in former years.' Malachi 3:4. Then the church which our Lord at His coming is to receive to Himself will be a 'glorious church, not having spot, or wrinkle, or any such thing.' Ephesians 5:27. Then she will look 'forth as the morning, fair as the moon, clear as the sun, and terrible as an army with banners.' Song of Soloman 6:10" (*The Great Controversy*, p. 425).

Personal Reflection and Discussion

1. What sequence of events does Daniel 12:1 describe?

_____

_____

2. How does Revelation 22:11, 12 depict the inhabitants of the earth just before Jesus returns?

_____

_____

3. What kind of relationship with Christ must His people have before the Second Coming?

_____

_____

4. How did Ellen White describe the purification time that is to take place before the judgment ends and Jesus arrives?

_____

_____

5. What role do the laws of physical, emotional, and spiritual health play in preparing for the end of time?

_____

Prayer Activity

- **Call your prayer partner and discuss this devotional with him/her.**
- **Pray with your prayer partner:**
    - **(1) for God to baptize you with His Holy Spirit.**
    - **(2) for God to help you and your family understand and practice the laws of physical, emotional, and spiritual health so that you can be ready for the end of the judgment and Christ's return.**
    - **(3) for the individuals on your prayer list.**

Day 40

A People Ready to Meet Jesus

Revelation 14 has three sections. The first deals with God's last-day people, the next with His last-day message, and the third with Christ's second coming. The first section, describing God's last-day people, appears in verses 1 through 5. "And I looked, and, lo, a Lamb stood on the mount Sion, and with him an hundred forty and four thousand, having his Father's name written in their foreheads. And I heard a voice from heaven, as the voice of many waters, and as the voice of a great thunder: and I heard the voice of harpers harping with their harps: And they sung as it were a new song before the throne, and before the four beasts, and the elders: and no man could learn that song but the hundred and forty and four thousand, which were redeemed from the earth. These are they which were not defiled with women; for they are virgins. These are they which follow the Lamb whithersoever he goeth. These were redeemed from among men, being the firstfruits unto God and to the Lamb. And in their mouth was found no guile: for they are without fault before the throne of God" (Rev. 14:1-5).

Notice several important characteristics about God's last-day people. They perfectly reflect the character of God and have the "Father's name written in their foreheads." This can happen only as they have followed principles of health, which cleared the way for God to manifest Himself in them fully in order to reflect His character in and through them. It is how God's glory will fill the earth just before Jesus returns. "And after these things I saw another angel come down from heaven, having great power; and the earth was lightened with his glory" (Rev. 18:1).

God's last-day people are "without fault" before Him. They will have the experience of Isaiah. "Then said I, woe is me! for I am undone; because I am a man of unclean lips. . . . Then flew one of the seraphims unto me, having a live coal in his hand, which he had taken with the tongs from off the altar: And he laid it upon my mouth, and said, Lo, this hath touched thy lips; and thine iniquity is taken away, and thy sin purged" (Isa. 6:5-7). God will take away all of our uncleanness, including such as anger and bitterness. He will heal us of all our wounds and hurts. Christ lives in us, and we will see others with the compassion and forgiving eye of Christ.

Since human beings have no righteousness of their own to make them faultless before God, last-day Christians accept the justifying and sanctifying righteousness of Christ. But to receive that, we must have Him living fully in us just as Paul described of himself: "I am crucified with Christ: nevertheless I live; yet not I, but Christ liveth in me: and the life which I now live in the flesh I live by the faith of the Son of God, who loved me, and gave himself for me" (Gal. 2:20).

Also God's last-day people will have experienced the completion of the "mystery of God" foretold in Revelation 10: "But in the days of the voice of the seventh angel, when he shall begin to sound, the mystery of God should be finished, as he hath declared to his servants the prophets" (verse 7). Paul informs us that the mystery of God is "Christ in you, the hope of glory" (Col. 1:27).

Following principles of good health in every area of our existence is essential for all these things to take place in our lives. Ellen White understood this when she wrote: "The body is the only medium through which the mind and the soul are developed for the up-building of character" (*The Ministry of Healing,* p. 130). It is vital that all Christians take seriously God's counsels on health if they want to be among those described in Revelation 14 and be ready for Christ's second coming.

Personal Reflection and Discussion

1. List the characteristics of God's last-day people described in Revelation 14:1-5.

_____
_____
_____
_____

2. Why is following the laws of physical health important in achieving these characteristics?

_____
_____

3. Why is following the laws of emotional health important in achieving these characteristics?

_____
_____

4. Why is following the laws of spiritual health important in achieving these characteristics?

_____
_____

5. What practices do you need to change in your life in order to achieve good physical, emotional, and spiritual health and be ready for Christ's second coming?

_____
_____

Prayer Activity

● **Call your prayer partner and discuss this devotional with him/her.**
● **Pray with your prayer partner:**
    (1) for God to baptize you with His Holy Spirit.
    (2) for God to help you and your family understand and practice the laws of health so that you can be among God's last-day people ready to meet Jesus.
    (3) for the individuals on your prayer list.

After 40 Days of Prayer and Devotional Studies

Now that you have completed the 40 days of prayer and devotional studies, you probably don't want the experience you are having with the Lord, and the fellowship you are enjoying, to fade away. So what should you do next?

One possibility is that you begin studying in greater detail the subjects presented in this devotional. Each section has been based on one of the books I have written. Their titles are:

The Baptism of the Holy Spirit
Spirit Baptism and Abiding in Christ
Spirit Baptism and Prayer
Spirit Baptism and Deliverance
Spirit Baptism and Earth's Final Events

I would suggest you start with the first book listed, *The Baptism of the Holy Spirit*, and begin studying it with your prayer partner or fellowship group who participated in the 40 days of prayer and devotional study with you. You may want to invite others to join you and your group. Then individually and as a group, continue to progress through each book. This will enable the Lord to strengthen the relationship with Him that He has begun in your life during the past 40 days.

Or if you haven't studied the first or second *40 Days* devotional, you could begin using one of them for your daily study.

Second, continue to pray for those on your prayer list and reach out to them. Also, add others to your list as the Lord leads, and as a group, consider activities to plan, and invite those on the prayer lists to attend.

Christ wants personal daily devotional study, prayer, and reaching out to others to become an integral part of every Christian's life. If this aspect of your life ends with the 40 days of prayer and devotional study, you will not grow into the fullness of Christ that He desires you to experience. In addition, it is the only way to be ready for Christ's soon return. For it is the only way our intimate relationship with Christ develops and grows. May the Lord abundantly bless your continued devotional study and prayer time with Him, and your efforts to share Him with others.

Note: All books listed are available through most Adventist Book Centers or at www.40daysdevotional.com.

vibrant life

www.vibrantlife.com

If you're determined to live a healthier and more energetic life, we're here to support you. Every issue of *Vibrant Life* encourages you to keep choosing better foods to eat. It provides vegetarian recipes that will attract the whole family. There's good advice on finding exercises that fit your lifestyle and natural remedies for the aches and pains that slow you down. *Vibrant Life* helps you stay on track--mentally, physically, and spiritually.

K22-01-0

mind   *body*   *spirit*

www.VibrantLife.com

vibrant life

America's First Health Magazine

Achieve a Healthy Mind, Body, and Spirit

▸ Two Words that Can Change Your Life

▸ How to Improve Your E.Q.

▸ 21 Tips for Spiritual Growth

▸ Healthy Recipes in 3 Steps or Less

Forks Over Knives

An exclusive interview with Dr. T. Colin Campbell, author of **The China Study**, and Dr. Caldwell Esselstyn, stars of the new blockbuster movie.

Could you do a marathon a day for 100 days?

Leo Schreven, 50, attempts the incredible!

May/June 2011

0 74470 19180 3

Call (800)456-3991 or order online at www.VibrantLife.com

ADDITIONAL RESOURCES

RECIPES TO REVERSE AND PREVENT:
· Obesity · High Blood Pressure
High Cholesterol · Diabetes · Heart Disease

IMPROVE YOUR HEALTH AND THE HEALTH OF YOUR FAMILY

The Optimal Diet
The Official CHIP Cookbook
Darlene Blaney and Hans Diehl

THE SUCCESSFUL LIFESTYLE-IMPROVEMENT program **CHIP** (Coronary Health Improvement Project) has now released a collection of their best recipes. Built on the goodness of natural foods, these delicious recipes will reverse and prevent obesity and disease. Improve your health while enjoying delicious food.
Hardcover, 166 pages. 978-0-8127-0437-2

Take Charge of Your Health
Aileen Ludington and Hans Diehl

THROUGH POWERFULLY motivating stories of changed lives the authors convey the rules for vibrant health, as well as how to shed bitterness, find new peace of mind, and recover a close connection with God. By simplifying their diet, eating unrefined foods, using natural remedies, and exercising health derelicts can become dynamos. Softcover, 144 pages. 978-0-8280-1559-2

You-Turn
Understanding, Preventing, and Reversing Lifestyle Diseases
Hans Diehl and Aileen Ludington

DO YOU WANT TO LIVE longer? live better? This little booklet outlines the causes of various lifestyle diseases and offers practical tips on how you can prevent, and even reverse, these debilitating conditions. Softcover, 62 pages. 978-0-8280-2448-8

Connect With Us

AVAILABLE IN BOOKSTORES AND FROM ONLINE RETAILERS

Availability subject to change.